Susan Cooper

Twayne's United States Authors Series

Ruth MacDonald, Editor

TUSAS 696

SUSAN COOPER
Photo by Paul Schneck Photography

Susan Cooper

Nina Mikkelsen

Twayne Publishers
An Imprint of Simon & Schuster Macmillan
New York

Prentice Hall International
London • Mexico City • New Delhi • Singapore • Sydney • Toronto

Twayne's United States Authors Series No. 696

Susan Cooper
Nina Mikkelsen

Copyright © 1998 by Twayne Publishers
All rights reserved. No part of this book may be reproduced or transmitted in any form or by any means, electronic or mechanical, including photocopying, recording, or by any information storage and retrieval system, without permission in writing from the Publisher.

Twayne Publishers
An Imprint of Simon & Schuster Macmillan
1633 Broadway
New York, NY 10019

Library of Congress Cataloging-in-Publication Data

Mikkelsen, Nina.
    Susan Cooper / Nina Mikkelsen.
        p. cm. — (Twayne's United States authors series ; TUSAS 696)
    Includes bibliographical references (p.   ) and index.
    ISBN 0-8057-7813-6 (alk. paper)
    1. Cooper, Susan—Criticism and interpretation. 2. Children's stories, American—History and criticism. 3. Fantastic fiction, American—History and criticism. 4. Children's stories, American—English influences. 5. Fantastic fiction, American—English influences. 6. Mythology, Celtic, in literature. 7. Time travel in literature. 8. Folklore in literature. I. Title. II. Series.
PS3553.06234Z76   1998
823'.914—dc21   97-35453
                                                                                 CIP

This paper meets the requirements of ANSI/NISO Z3948-1992 Permanence of Paper.

10 9 8 7 6 5 4 3 2 1

Printed in the United States of America

Contents

Preface ix
Acknowledgments xi
Chronology xiii

> *Chapter One*
> Childhood and Beyond   1
>
> *Chapter Two*
> The 1960s: Becoming a Children's Book Writer   7
>
> *Chapter Three*
> The 1970s: The *Dark Is Rising* Sequence (England)   24
>
> *Chapter Four*
> The *Dark Is Rising* Sequence (Wales)   49
>
> *Chapter Five*
> The *Dark Is Rising* Sequence and Readers   76
>
> *Chapter Six*
> After the *Dark Is Rising* Sequence   99
>
> *Chapter Seven*
> Susan Cooper as Writer   120

Notes and References   141
Selected Bibliography   146
Index   151

Preface

For the past three decades, through 15 books, Susan Cooper has been producing eloquent, insightful, and highly imaginative literature for children. She is best known for her modern fantasies involving mythical quests of present-day children, as seen most particularly in the *Dark Is Rising* sequence of five books. But she has proved her talents with a wide range of genres, from realistic fiction to fantasy of many different kinds, picture book or illustrated story, and drama (plays and teleplays). The settings for these genres cover an equally wide range, from Buckinghamshire to the Cornish coast of England and the high hills of Northern Wales, from the Western Highlands of Scotland to Toronto, and from the Chiltern Hills of England to the Caribbean Islands—in old time and new.

Cooper's work has often involved child characters traveling to earlier periods of historical and legendary time to encounter mythic figures who help initiate them into knowledge of good and evil. Her characters also include legendary creatures of the past ("little people" like the boggart) who find themselves transplanted into the present of the new world where they must deal with the confusing circumstances of modern times and places.

Her themes involve the quest to understand one's powers and use them for the good of the world—or the responsibility of knowledge—and the way the child as time-traveler (or the transplanted creature) adapts to sudden change in order to bring the greatest good to others. Her work stretches across several categories of modern fantasy (folk fantasy, time-travel, mythic or epic fantasy) and across every age group.

Although born and educated in England, Cooper has lived in America for the past 30 years, ever since her marriage in the early 1960s to an American professor. Americans have rewarded her with the Newbery Medal for *The Grey King* in 1976 and a Newbery Honor Award and the *Boston Globe-Horn Book* Award for *The Dark Is Rising* in 1974. She has also received two Horn Book Honor List Citations, the Tir na N'og Award (Wales) twice, a Carnegie Runner-Up Award, and a Carnegie Commendation (England) for various books of the *Dark Is Rising* sequence.

In this sequence, Cooper depicts children interacting with legendary British characters and engaging in heroic quests in which old and new are linked. In producing so many books in this particular type of fantasy, in which modern children discover personal and cultural knowledge through their encounters with supernatural figures of myth and legend, Cooper has carved out something of a genre all her own. One story weaves into another in her famous *Dark Is Rising* sequence, as characters of one book mingle with characters of another to form new books rising out of previous ones. And all of these books are linked by one major mythic figure (or constellation of figures of Arthurian legend).

Susan Cooper's ability to create engaging characters moving through highly evocative settings of both realistic and fantasy places of past and present, to take on large and important themes, to produce well-plotted, dramatic stories, and to do so with powerful language of strong cadence and visual imagery makes her a challenging and rewarding writer for readers of all ages, particularly children 9 to 12 years of age and beyond who find mythical quests, adventures, and conflicts so inviting. Her own transplanted state, from English and Welsh to American soil, produces an especially interesting case for biographical investigation.

This first book-length study of Susan Cooper recognizes an international children's writer in whom love of England and Wales and long residence in America have produced a highly imaginative blending. Her books have much to tell us about the human condition, about children, and about children's literature. This study of her work is designed to extend our awareness of the special talents she brings to readers.

Chapter 1 presents a biographical portrait of Susan Cooper as a child growing up during World War II in a London suburb in a small, close-knit English family in which the sharing of literature and her own early love of reading and writing produced a rich cauldron of stories from which she would later draw her own fiction.

Chapter 2 examines her fiction in chronological order of publication, beginning with *Over Sea, Under Stone,* the first book of the *Dark Is Rising* sequence, and *Dawn of Fear,* a book that can also serve as an introduction to the sequence.

Chapters 3 and 4 examine the sequence itself, beginning with the books set in England (*The Dark Is Rising* and *Greenwitch*), then moving on to the books set in Wales (*The Grey King* and *Silver on the Tree*). Chapter 5 focuses on reader reception of the sequence.

Chapter 6 concentrates on the fiction Cooper wrote after the sequence, from the 1980s to the present. Chapter 7 discusses Cooper as writer: the traditions and genres in which she works, her narrative processes and structures, and her vision of the world for children.

Because Susan Cooper has such a deep interest in and involvement with Celtic folk tradition, I have emphasized the relationship of her characters, themes, and narrative patterns to Celtic myths and legends. And I have discussed the way Cooper recreates stories of her own, based on these legends. She borrows; she invents; she reinvents, and the web of stories raying out of the main story reflects the many layers of cultural identity the books explore.

Acknowledgments

I would like to thank the following people for their generous help with this book: above all, Susan Cooper for writing the books and agreeing to this project, as well as for supplying photographs for this book and helpful correspondence; from Twayne Publishers: Mark Zadrozny for setting the book in motion, Ruth MacDonald for keeping it going, and Anne Davidson, and Impressions Book and Journal Services for ushering it through the publication process; Emma Dryden of McElderry Books for sending me advance copies of Susan Cooper's books; Derek Sanderson of Indiana, Pennsylvania, for sharing his responses to the *Dark Is Rising* sequence, February 1995; my son Vinny for giving me the book *Guinevere* and sending me down a new path for my research; my children, Vinny and Mark, at ages 13 and 11, for teaching me more about *The Dark Is Rising;* my husband, Vin, for accompanying me on so many quest-journeys in the field of children's literature, including this latest one to Mevagissey; and my mother, Martha Sullivan, and her sisters, Velma, Donna (Gehagen O'Sullivan), Miriam, Betty, Nancy, and Jean (Dilwyn Morgan), Celtic women all, for inspiring me to look more deeply into this part of my heritage.

Chronology

1935	Susan Mary Cooper born 23 May in Burnham, Buckinghamshire, England, first child of John Richard and Ethel May (Field) Cooper.
1953–1956	Wins state scholarship to Somerville College, Oxford University, majoring in English; becomes first woman to edit Oxford newspaper, *Cherwell*.
1956	Receives M.A., Somerville College, Oxford.
1956–1963	Reporter and feature writer for *Sunday Times,* London.
1963	Marries Nicholas J. Grant, American professor (divorced 1983). Moves to Winchester, Massachusetts.
1963–1972	Columnist for *Western Mail,* Cardiff, Wales ("Susan Cooper in America").
1964	*Mandrake* published.
1965	*Behind the Golden Curtain: A View of the USA* published. Book Society Alternative Choice in the United Kingdom. *Over Sea, Under Stone* published, named *Horn Book* honor list.
1966	Birth of son, Jonathan Roderick.
1967	Birth of daughter, Katharine Mary.
1970	*J. B. Priestley, Portrait of an Author* published. *Dawn of Fear* published in the United States, named ALA Notable Book, *Horn Book* honor list.
1973	*The Dark Is Rising* published, named ALA Notable Book, Newbery Honor Book, and Carnegie Medal runner-up; wins *Boston Globe-Horn Book* Award.
1974	*Greenwitch* published, named ALA Notable Book.
1975	*The Grey King* published, wins John Newbery Award, *Horn Book* Honor List, and ALA Notable Book Citation, Newbery Medal, Tir na N'og Award, and commendation for Carnegie Medal. Cooper recognized in *Who's Who in America*.
1977	*Silver on the Tree* published, wins Tir na N'og Award.

1979 *Jethro and the Jumbie* published.
1980 *Foxfire* (play) coauthored with Hume Cronyn, produced at Stratford, Ontario, in 1981, at the Guthrie Theater in Minneapolis, and in 1982 on Broadway at the Ethel Barrymore Theater.
1982 *Foxfire* published.
1983 *Seaward* published, wins B'nai B'rith Janusz Korczak Award.
1984 *The Dollmaker* (teleplay, in collaboration with Hume Cronyn, adaptation of novel *The Dollmaker* by Harriette Arnow), produced by American Broadcasting Company, 13 May; wins Christopher Award, Humanitas prize, Writers Guild of America Award, Emmy Award nomination for Academy of Television Arts and Sciences.
1985 *The Silver Cow,* illustrations by Warwick Hutton, published.
1986 *The Selkie Girl,* illustrations by Warwick Hutton, published; wins *Horn Book* Honor List citation.
1987 *Foxfire* (teleplay), produced by Hallmark for Columbia Broadcasting System, 13 December; wins Writers Guild of America Award and Emmy Award nomination.
1991 *Tam Lin,* illustrations by Warwick Hutton, published. *Matthew's Dragon,* illustrations by Joseph A. Smith, published.
1993 *Danny and the Kings,* illustrations by Joseph A. Smith, published. *The Boggart* published. *To Dance with the White Dog* (teleplay), adaptation of novel by Terry Kay, produced by Hallmark for Columbia Broadcasting System.
1996 Marries Hume Cronyn, 20 July. Moves to Fairfield, Connecticut. *Dreams and Wishes: Essays on Writing for Children* published.
1997 *The Boggart and the Monster* published.

Chapter One
Childhood and Beyond

From the beginning Susan Cooper was becoming a writer. Writing was in her genes, the times, and the many things she did to nurture her creative talents. Her maternal grandparents, the only grandparents she ever knew, are the ones she feels may have given her both the impulse and talent to write.

Frederick Benjamin Field, Susan's grandfather, was a "sturdy, upright Londoner with a noble nose and a tonsure of bushy white hair, a gentle patriarch to his seven children and nine grandchildren,"[1] and she would later use his image as Merriman Lyon in her *Dark Is Rising* sequence. A draper's assistant, he loved the theater, and the story was that his parents had been traveling players. He took his children to the first London production of *Peter Pan,* creating a tradition that Susan Cooper would later follow with her own children. At family parties he encouraged his grandchildren to perform poetry alongside his own recitations. He introduced Susan to his favorite novelists and took her to see a World War II film he especially liked, *A Matter of Life and Death,* made by Michael Powell and Emeric Pressburger, in 1946 (called *Stairway to Heaven* in the United States), which she has said became the strongest influence on her writing of anything she ever saw or read ("SC" 1988, 69).

Susan's grandmother, Mary Ellen Davies Field, from the fishing village of Aberdovey, was "small and quiet and Welsh" ("SC" 1988, 69). Cooper would later name one of her characters, Owen Davies (who is also small and quiet and Welsh), for her family name. "Perhaps I am a writer because of my grandmother's Welshness," says Cooper, "the Celtic blessing that turns itself often into the words or melody of song" ("SC" 1988, 69).

Mary Ellen came to London when her father, a sea captain in Aberdovey, drowned and her mother needed money to support the two younger children. At 14, she became a housemaid. Later she met and married Frederick Field, just as Ethel, one of their seven children, would later meet and marry another Londoner, John Richard Cooper. Susan Cooper's father was an amateur pianist who was fond of music and poetry, and he would occasionally "launch with spirit into a recitation of *La Belle Dame Sans Merci.*"[2] As a child, Susan heard and recited poetry in large quantities, and because "poetry, like fantasy, uses metaphor as its language," says Cooper, she is "by nature a poet who writes prose" ("SC" 1995, 168). Her mother, a teacher of 10-year-olds most of her life, taught Susan "from a head full of poetry [Tennyson, Browning, and the Romantic poets] and music and high standards" ("SC" 1988, 71). Cooper's mother, she says, was "loving, protective, and sympathetic" ("SC" 1988, 70), and it is perhaps Ethel Field Cooper whose personality flows through so many of the nurturing females of Cooper's fiction: Aunt Jen in *The Grey King;* Mrs. Stanton, Will's mother, in *The Dark Is Rising;* and Jane Drew in *Over Sea, Under Stone* and *Greenwitch*. Cooper's father was a gentle, blue-eyed man with an office job that he hated at the Great Western Railway, and each summer the family took its holiday in Cornwall, just as she would portray it in *Over Sea, Under Stone* and *Greenwitch*. Susan had a younger brother, just as young Jane Drew, in these books, did. And they all waited through the long hours aboard the train for "the first magical sight of the sea." Her father "would become like a boy himself at the sight of it," and her mother "would take care of [them] all" ("SC" 1988, 70).

The Cooper family spent summer holidays in Wales; Aberdovey "tugged at" her mother, she says, "being full of relations."[3] But Susan visited there at other times as well. She was often ill as a child and went there for convalescences, as Will does in *The Grey King*. As the Welsh genes took over, she became "totally obsessed with the place, with the hills and the sea and the village in between" ("MLW," 80). Her roots are in Wales, she says, and she is "haunted" by it. And "if you're a writer," she adds, "it's that kind of haunting that shapes your imagination" ("MLW," 80).

Cooper has theorized that writers are "controlled by one particular period" in their lives. "All the feelings and sights and sounds are sucked fiercely into the imagination as if it's a sponge, and they never go away. It can be at any period in life," this "unconscious absorbing," but for her it was "sometime between the ages of 4 [when World War II began] and 10 [when the war ended]," and it occurred in Wales. There she gained "a sense of place, a sense of race and therefore a leaning toward a particular kind of myth and legend and otherness which the Welsh have about the English" ("MLW," 80).

"One race after another lived in these islands for hundreds of years at a time, and then found itself driven westwards by some fearsome bloody-minded invaders," she says. "Wales, then, is the place where my ancestors were driven back but never driven out so it's home" ("MLW").

Wales affected the stories she wrote as she was growing up and the way she responded to stories she heard, and later it would echo through the stories she wrote as an adult, especially the books of the *Dark Is Rising* sequence and the "theme of echoing myth" ("MLW," 80) that she has become famous for weaving through her work.

When Cooper was ready for college, her parents moved from England to Wales, where they lived for 20 years, and so she continued to spend holidays there. Yet when she thought, " 'I want to go home,' "[4] the place she pictured was her childhood home in Huntercombe, Buckinghamshire, England, the background of Will Stanton's adventures in *The Dark Is Rising,* Cooper's own peaceful "refuge in a world of distress and threat" (*DW,* 88) during World War II and the place depicted in such meticulous detail in her autobiographical novel, *Dawn of Fear.*

Buckinghamshire is 23 miles from London, and from their home the Coopers could hear the air-raid sirens, feel the earth shake from the bombings, and see the German machine gunners sweeping down from a dull red sky when London was burning in the Blitz. The noise, the broken glass, the air-raid warnings, the trek down into the "cold steel-roofed cave dug into the back lawn" ("SC" 1988, 67), and the house down the street that had been blown away—all of this turned the child Susan into an adult who would jump at loud noises, catch her breath at the sound of a siren, and stand shaking before audiences to whom she spoke about her fiction.

When Susan was 10 years old, the strain of war caused her father to suffer a nervous collapse (what we today might call clinical depression, although he was neither diagnosed nor treated). He nearly committed suicide one night when the effect of two wars overwhelmed him, and he came home only because of his family. (He was only 18 years old when he was sent off to World War I and was shot through the leg.) Home was his refuge and to Susan, "an abnormally shy child," as she describes in her memoir, *Dreams and Wishes,* "home also took on abnormally large importance as a place of emotional security" (*DW,* 88).

Writing also became a refuge. By the time of her father's illness, she had written three plays for a neighbor's puppet theater, had collaborated with another child on a weekly newspaper, and had written a fairy tale. She had developed confidence in her writing by the time she went to Oxford. There she attended lectures by C. S. Lewis and J. R. R. Tolkien, became immersed in Spenser and Malory, and wrote a minithesis entitled "Shakespeare's Treatment of Time" (*DW,* 183). She published her first short story. She also wrote for the *Cherwell,* the Oxford University newspaper, and later she would become its first female editor. Her Oxford years were good ones, and during her last term she wrote about them for a piece published by the London *Times*.

Soon she was on her way, working two jobs in London, one as a temporary reporter for the *Sunday Express,* the other a small job in a publishing house. It was the mid-1950s, and she was earning eight pounds a week until she lost the reporting job when she failed to produce her assigned story about Marilyn Monroe during Monroe's stay in London. A more aggressive (or foolhardy) reporter might have scaled the police-protected wall of the house where Monroe and Arthur Miller were staying as newlyweds. But Cooper had no stomach for such intrusive behavior. Discharged from the *Express,* she found a new job at the *Sunday Times,* working for none other than Ian Fleming, "[t]all, handsome, elegant, and courteous," as she recalls, and who would disappear "from time to time to write another James Bond novel in his house in Jamaica" ("SC" 1988, 73).

Eventually she became a reporter and feature writer for the *Sunday Times,* where she learned how to tell a story in two hundred words or "flesh it out in five thousand"; became acquainted with "all manner of subjects in hundreds of different parts of Britain"; and met film stars, politicians, "janitors, and garbagemen" ("SC" 1988, 73). Because she did not like the journalistic constrictions on length, she began writing her own books in her spare time. And for fun and to nurture her love of myth and folktale, she wrote feature articles on King Arthur and Roman Britain.

In her mid-twenties, she found herself the author of a science fantasy for adults, *Mandrake,* and the first book of the *Dark Is Rising* sequence, *Over Sea, Under Stone.* All of this came about in one year, the same year she saw her picture on a 15-foot-high billboard in Piccadilly Circus (London's Times Square), which was advertising a feature series she was producing. This shy writer responded to the publicity by taking off for America as the wife of an American engineer 19 years her senior and the father of three teenage children.

Winchester, Massachusetts, became a quiet refuge. There in an attic study that her new husband created for her, she could watch the squirrels and write about American life. She submitted special features to the *Sunday Times,* covering such topics as the Jack Ruby trial in Dallas; contributed a weekly column to the *Western Mail* in Wales; and penned a book of essays, *Behind the Golden Curtain,* explaining America to the English. Two babies, Jon (1966) and Kate (1967), were soon on the way, as well as two more nonfiction books, an edited collection of J. B. Priestley's essays, and a biography of Priestley, a novelist and playwright whose wife, archaeologist Jacquetta Hawkes, had written *The Land,* a book Cooper had read earlier and remembered as an important influence.

Priestley himself also had a significant effect on her as a writer and friend. Consoling her in her homesickness for England, he advised her: " 'Don't worry about living abroad. You'll find you write better about a place when you're away from it' " ("SC" 1988, 77). And she did. Soon, in *Dawn of Fear,* she was telling the story of her wartime childhood and then launching into her *Dark Is Rising* sequence, in which the child protagonist was named Will, "after the most remarkable Englishman of all" ("SC" 1988, 78). Each book took at least a year to write, and this was a happy and peaceful stretch of time for her, living with her real family and her invented one. She wrote while at home in Massachusetts and at their vacation home in the British Virgin Islands. With her back to the sea and her mind in England, she wrote much of the *Dark Is Rising* sequence. Moreover, while in the islands she was to meet a man who would affect her life greatly in the coming years.

In 1974, when Cooper had just flown to New York to receive a Newbery Honor Award for *The Dark Is Rising,* Hume Cronyn and his wife, Jessica Tandy, were also staying in the islands. That was the beginning, Cooper related in the late 1980s, "of a communal friendship and—eventually—working relationship that hasn't ended yet, and a great deal of talk about the theatre, and the double occupation of storytelling and entertainment in which both actors and writers are involved" ("SC" 1988, 80).

Susan Cooper and Hume Cronyn would go on to collaborate on a play called *Foxfire,* which was produced on Broadway, and a teleplay, *The Dollmaker,* both winners of numerous prestigious awards. Their collaboration, as she predicted, has not ended yet. In 1996, some years after Cooper's divorce in the early 1980s and following Jessica Tandy's death in 1994, Susan and Hume were married. What this talented and versatile couple will create for the American stage, television, or film worlds in the future, only time will tell. At this point she is rewriting a television script of Anne Tyler's *Dinner at the Homesick Restaurant* and composing a film script for the book *The Boggart* as she travels with her husband between Los Angeles, where he is acting in a film, and their home in Connecticut.[5]

Cooper's cross-cultural heritage also sends her back to Britain at least once a year to see family and friends, especially her brother Rod, who is editor of the regional magazine "Kent Life" and father of two children, Richard James and Naomi Susan. Susan and Rod each named one of their children for the other, and Susan also dedicated to Rod her autobiographical novel, *Dawn of Fear* (1970), which she wrote when her children (Jonathan Roderick and Katharine Mary) were toddlers.

Each of her children is now grown. With degrees from Cornell, the University of Florida, and MIT, Jon is an ocean engineer (and a "dedicated oarsman," she says) with a consulting firm in Cambridge, Massachusetts. After obtaining a degree in Russian from Connecticut College, spending a year in the Ukraine, and completing the Radcliffe University intensive publishing course, Kate now lives in Boston and works in book production. "Both children," says Cooper, "are wonderful people, and more valuable to me than all the books in the world."[6]

Cooper has written about her children's reading interests, reading habits, and responses to literature in many of her essays. It may be her close observation of and involvement with her own children that have brought special insight into child culture as depicted in so much of her work. Since completing the *Dark Is Rising* sequence in 1977, she has gone on to explore picture books, young adult coming-of-age fantasy, and contemporary folk fantasy for young readers featuring a mischievous creature of the Old Magic, the boggart. A new Susan Cooper has emerged in the 1990s with *The Boggart* and a companion book, *The Boggart and The Monster,* two humorous and thought-provoking fantasies about a Scottish "little person."

If we consider the entire collection of her work thus far, we see a serious and eloquent author of High Fantasy and a witty and stimulating creator of contemporary folk fantasy. We begin with the earlier Susan Cooper and gradually make our way to the later one in order to learn more about this multifaceted writer.

Chapter Two
The 1960s: Becoming a Children's Book Writer

In the 1960s, Susan Cooper was a journalist, novelist, biographer, essayist, wife, mother, and children's book writer. But it is two early works of fiction—*Over Sea, Under Stone,* 1965, and *Dawn of Fear,* 1970—that will concern us here, since these books both serve as something of a prelude to the famous *Dark Is Rising* sequence.

In the late 1950s and early 1960s, Cooper was working as a reporter and feature writer for the *Sunday Times* in London, as well as writing fiction in her spare time. Her earliest novel was never published. Two other novels were published in England in the mid-1960s, after she had moved to Massachusetts. The first to reach print was *Mandrake* (1964), a science fantasy for adults that satirized British thinking in the postwar and Cold War era. The second was *Over Sea, Under Stone* (1965), a book that began as a children's adventure story but evolved as a quest fantasy for readers of any age because of its focus on the King Arthur legends Cooper loved as a child.

Over Sea, Under Stone

When Cooper was 25 years old and working in London as a feature writer for the *Sunday Times,* the paper's literary editor encouraged her to try writing a "family adventure story" (*DW,* 7) for a contest held in honor of writer E. Nesbit. It sounded like fun to Cooper, so she jumped in, inventing three siblings—Simon, Jane, and Barney Drew, who were involved in a quest in southern Cornwall for a grail dating back to Arthurian times. Ultimately she forgot about the contest when the quest images that had "haunted" her since childhood began taking over the story (*DW,* 7).

The book does sometimes echo E. Nesbit's trilogy, *Story of the Amulet, Five Children and It,* and *Phoenix and the Carpet,* which involves the adventures of a quartet of siblings (one of whom is named Jane). Like Nesbit's Jane, Cooper's young female is courteous and reserved yet spirited and always sensitive to the feelings of others. And in many ways her older brother, Simon, well grounded in the study of Latin, and her younger brother, Barney, so knowledgeable about the Arthurian legends, are at least "second cousins," in their speech, thoughts, and behavior, to Nesbit's precocious siblings Cyril and Robert. Who are Cooper's children really? The extended family of E. Nesbit—or something else?

Characters

From an upper-middle-class London family, the Drew children have a physician father and an artist mother, as well as a close friend of the family called Great-Uncle Merry, who looks and acts more like an exotic grandfather or a wizard than the professor he is. Merriman Lyon (Uncle Merry) eventually comes to signify, at least to Barney, the legendary wizard Merlin, who taught the child Arthur what he knew about the magic arts, as T. H. White reveals in *The Sword in the Stone*.

The Drew children are perceptive, responsible, and dedicated to the quest in which they quickly become immersed. The name Drew may bring to mind the ancient Celtic caste of intellectual leaders and wise people—the Druids—although there was no such link in Cooper's mind when she created the book.

To these children, Uncle Merry entrusts the mission of finding a grail or chalice that was hidden long ago for safekeeping and now needs to come to light for the sake of mankind. As he explains: " '[I]f the grail, that is the last trust of the old world, be not lost, then when the day is over the Pendragon [King Arthur] shall come again.' "[1]

Arthur " 'wasn't altogether beaten,' " Merriman tells the children, but he did not altogether win, so the struggle between good and evil has continued ever since. And " 'those men who remembered the old world have been searching for its secret ever since,' " he adds. " 'And there have been others searching as well—the enemies, the wicked men, who have the same greed in their cold hearts as the men whom Arthur fought' " (*OSUS*, 72).

With echoes of fantasy emanating from him, it gradually becomes clear that Merriman may be more than merely a professor: "Great-Uncle Merry looked out into the distance, his head outlined against the sky like the proud carved head of a statue, centuries old and yet always the same. 'I have been searching,' he said. 'For many, many years.' The children stared at him, awed and a little afraid. For a moment he was a stranger, someone they did not know" (*OSUS*, 72).

Jane has a "sudden fantastic feeling" (*OSUS,* 72) that their great-uncle does not really exist and might even vanish if they utter a word. In this book and the ones to come, he does often disappear and reappear for reasons these children are rarely privileged to know. He is (or becomes in later books) a spirit, a Celtic shaman or shape changer, one who navigates the world and the ages as a time-traveler. But in this book, less fantastic than the others, he is more easily seen as Great-Uncle Merry than as Merlin, for this is a book that moves along like the little boats that sail from the Trewissick harbor, largely on the power of realistic scene building.

Structure

Over Sea, Under Stone is divided into 13 untitled chapters and an epilogue, but perhaps more relevant are its several highly visual scenes, or scene-clusters (discovery of the manuscript; the story of the grail; Simon's escape; moonlight on Kemare Head; carnival; finding the grail; and losing the "pattern"). As Cooper wrote this book, she brought together her own childhood recollection of the Arthurian legends and family adventure stories such as those Nesbit wrote. In the first scene of *Over Sea, Under Stone,* the children find an old manuscript one rainy afternoon when they are exploring secret passages in the sea captain's house in Cornwall, where they are spending their summer vacation. Behind a wardrobe in one of the bedrooms that has been closed off for years, they discover not the magical world that C. S. Lewis's Lucy discovered in the Narnia books but the remnants of one. In an old parchment covered with strange writing and a drawing that resembles a map, Barney deciphers the names King Arthur and Mark, King of Cornwall. Great-Uncle Merry tells them about Arthur the Pendragon (*Pen* meaning *son of* and *dragon* meaning *chief*) and the struggle of good and evil in the world. He then reads from the parchment a monk's tale about a knight named Bedwin, who fled to Cornwall 900 years ago with a grail that told the "true story of Arthur" (*OSUS,* 74) in word and picture inscriptions. If this grail is not lost, the parchment promises, the Pendragon will return someday when the time is right.

The monk says that he himself is old and childless and terror reigns again in his own day, so he, too, must flee (north into Wales, the parchment implies). But, according to legend, the grail must remain in England to await Arthur. Simon, the doer, the child with a scientific bent, wants to know what a grail is (a cup or chalice, but not an ordinary one, Uncle Merry explains). Barney, a student of Arthurian lore and budding artist, realizes that the map is actually a picture of the headland where they sit listening, with the harbor below and the 3000-year-old standing stones farther out on the headland. Jane, the empathetic one, says nothing. She simply sits "thinking of the sad Cornishman sailing away over the sea from his threatened land" (*OSUS*, 76).

The children's task is to find the grail, when others, with less altruistic motives, are searching for it, too: Mr. Hastings, impersonating a vicar; Bill, a young Cornish boy related to the Drews' housekeeper; Mr. Withers, supposedly an antique dealer; and his sister Polly. (It is no coincidence that Cooper was writing this book in the early 1960s, 900 years after the Norman victory over the Saxons at the Battle of Hastings [1066], when the knight Bedwin came "fleeing towards the west" [*OSUS*, 71] [Cornwall]. It is also no accident that Hastings and Norman Withers, who sells antiques, are now trying to recover a most important antique, the grail that Bedwin brought with him.)

The children find themselves preyed upon and constantly intimidated by their adversaries. In fact, in each of the remaining dominant scenes of the book, the members of this "dark" quartet loom ominously over the children in order to seize the manuscript. They chase Simon around the village one day. They terrorize Simon and Jane one night as they stand on Kemare (King Mark) Head, and they kidnap Barney at the village carnival in order to gain more information about the grail. They threaten the children's lives the day the youngsters finally discover the grail and a second manuscript hidden deep in the rock cavern of Kemare Head. And the manuscript, which has the key for deciphering the verse pattern on the side panel of the grail, is lost.

Emotional Resonance

Cooper's scenes produce a clear and evocative picture of a character's action or feelings and of a landscape filled with menacing evil. Consider Simon, running with the manuscript from Bill, the Cornish boy, and Bill's "master," Hastings, both of whom are trying to wrestle it from him, and the way the scene dramatizes the tension of the chase and Simon's strong need to carry out his mission, as well as the heavy burden this task is placing on a *child's* shoulders. These scenes are also filled with a variety of literary "echoes" that produce a richly textured work for child readers.

The picture of Simon running is filtered through words we may or may not recall or associate with T. S. Eliot's poem "Burnt Norton,"[2] a favorite work of Cooper's, but the effect is the same: a stronger sense of dramatic action and emotional resonance:

> Lost me, thought Simon with a grin. His terror faded as their footsteps died away . . . There was silence again now, and he could hear nothing but the song of the birds in the approaching dusk . . . Clutching the manuscript firmly, he parted the bushes before his face with one hand and stepped out into the drive. No one was there. Nothing moved . . . It was not until he was several paces out in the open that he saw the boy Bill and the dark man standing together beside the wall fifty yards away, in clear view. Simon gasped, and felt his stomach twist with panic . . . Down the side road, round the corner and along the wall of the churchyard, faster, faster; Simon's heart sank as he ran. His legs were stiff after the cramped pause in the bushes, and his whole body was very tired. He knew that he would not be able to last very much longer . . . His breath began to come in great painful gasps, and he staggered as he ran . . . He heard the boy call, on a note of triumph: 'Quick . . . *now* . . .' The voice was farther away than the footsteps. (*OSUS*, 100–101)

All Uncle Merry can offer Simon at the end of his mission are the words " 'It was very well done' " (*OSUS*, 103). But this is also the best gift he can offer; it enables the child to assume the adult role with more confidence, especially when the children echo his encouragement, saying to Simon in turn, " 'Oh well done' " (*OSUS*, 103). The phrase (from Prospero's words to Ariel and the other spirits in Shakespeare's *The Tempest*) is one we will hear often in Cooper's books. It is not simply praise. It is more than mere encouragement. It implies intuitive understanding of a person's efforts, in this case, the courage it took to get the job done. It implies empathy and the ability to put aside personal accomplishments in order to acknowledge others' achievements for the greater good.

Cooper's ability to create a landscape filled with menacing evil is also evident in the moonlight scene on Kemare Head. Here Cooper uses Jane to exemplify the state of terror, beset as she is by the figure of Hastings, looming near on this dark night, when Merry is nowhere to be found. (He has simply vanished, as she earlier imagined him doing.) And again there are literary echoes that produce texture and resonance; this time Cooper chooses, aptly enough, the Old English epic poem *Beowulf:* "Straight as an arrow the long white road of the moon's reflection stretched toward them across the surface of the sea, like a path from the past and a path to the future; at its edges it danced and glimmered as the waves rose beneath the wind. And where it ended, at the tip of Kemare Head, a clear dark silhouette stood against the shining sea-carried light" (*OSUS,* 117).

At this moment what the children see tells them that "the grail must be hidden somewhere in that clump of rocks. Buried on the end of Kemare Head" (*OSUS,* 117). Illuminating the children's thinking, the moon also casts light on the "tall dark shape" of a man (Hastings), who towers over them in a great cloak, with "dark jutting brows" (*OSUS,* 119), causing Jane to scream.

Simon retains his composure, appearing "much braver than he felt" (*OSUS,* 118) as Merriman appears to sweep Jane up "as if she had been a baby" (*OSUS,* 119) and usher the children quickly home. Thus Jane appears as the stereotypical dependent female. She has stood "speechless with fright" (*OSUS,* 118); she has later screamed and been called stupid by Simon when she warns him away from the standing stones. Feeling safe once again, she has sobbed with relief. And it does not really lessen her dependency that, as the narrator says, "If she had not been there Simon would have been as paralyzed by fright himself" (OSUS, 118), since his presence merely encourages her to show her emotions freely. (As a female, she is expected to be emotional; thus her feelings are emphasized more than if another, more reserved female were present to offset them.)

Cooper thus gains and loses by placing only one female into her triad of child characters, as opposed to the quartet of two males and two females that E. Nesbit uses in her family adventure stories. Since shy, tearful Jane is the only female child here, Cooper forgoes the possibility of creating a brave, independent, nonquivering female. But she gains in that many young readers can take comfort in Jane's rational thinking: The reason she has been so frightened by the tall, dark figure in the moonlight is that she knew who he was. He is the same man she had met at the old vicarage and had assumed was the vicar, the one who won her trust so that he could study the old guidebook and map of the village she has discovered.

Also, Jane is younger than Simon, so when she is carried like a "baby," she is seen more as the young child than the female child. Had Cooper produced a female as the youngest child, rather than a male (Barney), the role of brave, adventuresome female would have been well met. But in strong-willed, daring, artistic Barney, she also creates a deeper, more individualized, more sensitive, portrait of a boy.

Barney sees with the artist's eye, and it is his strong imagination that carries him through the most challenging part of the quest, the time when he must have both courage and determination to proceed deeper and deeper into the cave to find the grail (he is the shortest and smallest sibling and can squeeze into tight places). What gives him the ability to keep going is the memory of Hastings's face the day this man ordered Polly Withers and her brother to kidnap him: the scowl, the grim lines, the coldness.

The deeper into the cave he goes, the colder and more frightened he becomes. His ears sing with voices telling him to retreat (his imagination at work), but then he remembers Uncle Merry's story of the knight Bedwin: "In full armour he stood in Barney's mind, guarding the last trust of King Arthur. Chased by the same forces that were now pursuing them. And Barney remembered the story that Bedwin was buried on Kemare Head, perhaps directly above the cave where he stood, and he was not frightened. There was friendliness round him in the dark now as well as fear" (*OSUS,* 195).

Thematic Focus

This is Barney's quest we see; it is particularly the *children's* quest. And what Cooper achieves most of all in her male-female-male configuration of children is a generic family unit. As the older siblings, Simon and Jane have important parts to play. They form a protective paternal/maternal scaffolding for Barney as "only" child in this quest. Simon runs with the manuscript before Polly Withers can grab it, Jane having screamed just in time to warn him. And each of them devises the theories that set the quest in motion and propel it to completion.

But it is Barney who has the courage, the trust, and the will power that only a child would have to complete the mission when others become fainthearted. Simon and Jane, in their conventional wisdom, decide that since they are trapped by the rising tide and their enemies have suddenly appeared in Withers's yacht, there is nothing to do but give in—and give up the quest. Barney, however, grabs both the grail and the little lead case they found with it (the second manuscript) and faces down the enemy. "The whole world seemed to stop and centre round the towering black-clad man and a small boy: one will against another, with Barney saved by his own fury from the full force of the commanding glare driving into his eyes" (*OSUS*, 208). He holds out until the moment Merriman comes charging up in a speedboat and Simon can grab back the grail and throw it to him.

They are not so lucky with the little case, which Simon has dropped into the center of the larger telescope case containing the parchment and which Jane has steadied with her handkerchief to prevent the frail paper from crumbling. Withers rises in the dinghy to stab the case in midflight with an oar, sending it soaring into the air, where the two halves spin apart, the little lead case splashing "like a stone into the sea" (*OSUS*, 211) and the shredding parchment disappearing in the waves. Only Jane's handkerchief is left "bobbing forlornly on the waves" (*OSUS*, 211), bringing to mind the Desdemona complex that emanates from Jane's character in this book. Innocent, generous, self-forgetful, amiable, and essentially or traditionally feminine (intuitive, nurturing, at times fearful, and happy to be protected by a patriarchal figure), she suffers wrongs in stoic silence, with only the handkerchief to signal the utter loss or ruin of the quest at this point.

Layers of identity nestle in the embedded stories of the handkerchief, as in Shakespeare's *Othello*. If Desdemona lost the handkerchief or gave it away, matchless "perdition" would result since there is "magic in the web of it," as Othello tells Desdemona. (Dyed from the fluid of maidens' hearts, a sibyl in prophetic fury had stitched it together.) The magic is the postmodernist intertextual web Cooper is spinning both to utilize and subvert the Desdemona syndrome. For although Barney feels gloomy, saying they have failed in their quest, and Simon feels bitter, thinking about how close they came to saving the case, it is Jane, resourceful and wise, who remembers the place where she was standing when the case disappeared into the water and where they can later look (Mr. Penhallow had told them earlier that such big tides usually come in March and September). With Jane's information, everyone, including the all-knowing Merriman, has hope for reversing the ill-fated quest.

So for now, the secret of the second manuscript is safe in the waterproof lead case, Merry assures them, safe from the sea and safe from their enemies on land. If they go back to search for it in the spring, when the tides are low again, they will know where to start looking: in the deep pool in the rocks.

In the epilogue we learn that the grail, placed now in the British Museum by Uncle Merry, contains five panels. On its last panel are words that correspond to those of the second manuscript, now lost.

Scholars passing before the exhibit, where the children are standing, see the words as runic, but of what culture (Saxon, Celtic, Scandinavian, Roman) they cannot agree, although the words appear to produce proof of a Celtic Arthur rather than an Arthur of Saxon, Roman, or Danish heritage. And since the second manuscript is the key and it is not there, the mystery remains unsolved.

What is the "real truth about King Arthur" (*OSUS*, 221), the children wonder as the story ends. Who was he? What happened to him? What was the secret of King Arthur that his enemies wanted—and still want? Things draw to a close with Barney's prophecy that the time will come when they *will* know, and it is easy to speculate that as Cooper finished the book, she had ideas for a sequel.

Greenwitch, a book she would not publish until nine years later, is so similar to this book in form and arrangement that it is difficult not to think that it was already in the works much earlier. It lacks only the character of Will Stanton, who was included in the cast of *Greenwitch* after Cooper wrote *The Dark Is Rising* and decided to create a set of sequels to *Over Sea, Under Stone*. In 1976 she wrote: "I had no intention then of writing a sequel to *Over Sea, Under Stone*—though I did leave it open-ended, since I'd grown fond of the characters, especially the Merlin-figure called Merriman, and I didn't want to cut myself off from them forever" (*DW,* 7).

But she did not take the sequel path immediately. Her next book turned completely away from Arthurian legends, quest fiction, and family adventure. *Dawn of Fear,* the story of Cooper's own childhood during World War II, was realistic fiction, without any echoes of fantasy whatsoever. In some ways it is—or at least began and remained to some degree—fiction for adult readers or what might be called "literature of child culture," rather than simply children's literature, which, of necessity, depicts child culture.

In a thematic genre such as literature of child culture, adults in fiction tell the stories of their own childhood as they define, illuminate, or explore what it means to be a child in a particular time, place, and culture. Penelope Lively's *Going Back,* Alice Walker's *To Hell With Dying,* Amy Tan's *Moon Lady,* and Peter Sis's *Three Golden Keys* all exemplify this genre. The characters may be children, and readers may be seeing things through the eyes of a child protagonist, but the preoccupations are those of adults exploring childhood from an adult perspective, and these books are often less successful with child readers as a result. Nina Bawden's *Carrie's War,* which exhibits traits of this category, still focuses on children's preoccupations for the most part, as does Cooper's book. Thus both books have been successful with both child and adult readers.

Dawn of Fear

Six years after Cooper's arrival in America, she was 34 years old and the mother of two young children. Did she want to write more children's books like *Over Sea, Under Stone*? It never occurred to her to do so, she says. "There were so many other good books by other people, for small children."[3] Instead she continued writing just for herself and for the child she had been, since the world of that child had left its mark, or more precisely, some deep scars. Each day when her children were asleep or at nursery school, she found herself writing what she now calls her "war book" (*DW,* 139), a fictional autobiography of her childhood years living on the outskirts of London when air raids, bombings, and the death of friends and neighbors were something of a daily routine.

Characters and Intertextual References

Originally called "The Camp," *Dawn of Fear* is about "a child's gradual discovery that war is not exciting and heroic but terrible" (*DW,* 139). Composed of nine days as the nine chapters, it takes place in a 13-day period. The story begins on a Friday, a school day when an air raid interrupts things, and three friends, Derek, Peter, and Geoff, are in no hurry to scurry into the shelter because it is so exciting to watch planes battling in the sky.

Through Derek's eyes we see the story, and since he is actually Susan herself, as Cooper has explained, the book blends two points of view—Derek's and an adult narrator's—and three genres: historical fiction (it is set in Cooper's own childhood of the 1940s), realistic fiction (Cooper attempts to record Derek's everyday experiences, thoughts, and feelings with unwavering precision), and autobiography. "Every word" of the story, Cooper says, is a "recording of events that actually happened" (*DW,* 139), except a few, like the fact that it all actually happened to a female—Susan—rather than to a male—Derek.

Derek's two friends are males, similar to Cooper's closest childhood friends—the Peter and Geoff characters here. "[T]here were no children in any of those families to be friends with," as Derek (Susan) reflects in the novel, "only babies and one small unthinkable girl their own age, with long golden hair, a high whining voice, and a small baby carriage over which she could sometimes be seen leaning in the distance, on the pavement outside her own house, talking to dolls."[4]

The next day is Saturday, and Derek visits Peter, sharing Peter's excitement about his family's new indoor bomb shelter called a "Morrison." (Derek's family's shelter is "planted" more traditionally underground in the back garden.) Risk-taking and curious, Peter is something of a Peter Rabbit figure in human form. He is "an unworried boy," says the narrator, "more often in trouble than any of them, but always a carefree kind of trouble" (*DF,* 23).

Returning home from Peter's house, Derek listens to one of the *Just So Stories* of Rudyard Kipling, "The Cat That Walked by Himself." Coming after the narrator's description of Peter, the Kipling story serves to juxtapose Peter, Peter Rabbit, and the cat as three of a kind: independent, brave, and persevering. And the words Cooper takes from Kipling, foreshadowing all that is to come, mark the theme of her story, too: "*Hear and attend and listen; for this befell and behappened and became and was, O my Best Beloved, when the Tame animals were wild*" (*DF,* 26).

That night Derek's father shows him a red sky. London is burning, he says, an incident Cooper also describes in her memoirs. "They were Londoners," she explains. "They wanted us to remember" (*DW,* 14). Derek's parents continue talking; they want to teach their children to be careful but not afraid. Derek's father says he hopes nothing will happen to make Derek learn fear for himself. "Fear is my personal legacy of war," says Cooper. "I've been fighting it all my life, often without success: fear of the dark, fear of deep water, fear of large gatherings of people . . . It's really an unattached, almost abstract fear that I'm talking about" (*DW,* 142).

The following day, Sunday, the six children who live on White Road (down the street from Derek's family) appear. The two gangs habitually avoid one another, just as their parents have no contact with each other, although "nobody seemed to know why" (*DF,* 31), as the narrator of the story says. The only child of the White Road gang given a name is David Wiggs, and one of the intriguing blank spaces of the book is what this dreadful child and his older brother represent in terms of the child culture being portrayed—or in the wider world at large, since the two gangs ultimately appear as microcosmic images of the Allies and Axis powers at war in the European theater.

As the story unfolds, we see David Wiggs, a "weasely boy in a dirty gray sweater" (*DF,* 37), torturing a cat; later, with the other gang members, he will steal from Peter, kill the cat, and destroy the camp that

Derek and his friends have made. His older brother, Johnny, will be revealed as a draft dodger (not an insignificant matter in this war) who sells things on the black market. Moreover, their father, a truck driver, is labeled lazy by the neighbors because of his unkempt property. What is the Wiggs family intended to represent? David Wiggs's speech patterns (" 'I been watching for you. I got something to give you' " [*DF,* 155]) may indicate that a rural or provincial area is slowly being encroached upon or turned into a London suburb, with families of different socioeconomic backgrounds suddenly being forced together (thus the antagonism). However, the constellation of character traits—neglectfulness of property, deliberate cruelty to animals, disdain for the law, lack of patriotism, laziness, slovenliness, nonstandard speech patterns, and vandalism—is particularly puzzling. The Wiggs family may be members of a lower economic class than the children of Derek's group, or they may simply be untidy, improvident people of whatever class. Nevertheless, class alone, or slovenly behavior by members of any class, would not instigate the "evil" that exudes from the Wiggs brothers.

When the two gangs encounter one another on this day, Derek stands paralyzed when he sees David Wiggs strangling a cat. This instance of blatant aggression foreshadows an important character in Cooper's fiction generally: the bully who must be stopped. We have seen him in *Over Sea, Under Stone* in the Cornish boy Bill, who knocks Jane off her bike and never expresses remorse (Jane called him *beastly*). And we will see him in *Silver on the Tree,* when Richie Moore intimidates Manny Singh, a Sikh boy, by throwing his violin in the stream. There the Indian immigrant as "outside" child replaces the cat as victim.

Sometimes the "he" is a "she," as in another story Cooper tells about her childhood. In "Muffin,"[5] Daisy (who is neither Derek nor Susan, Cooper says, but a classmate of theirs) is bullied by a character called "Fat Alice," a "big, pasty-faced girl," with a "high, whiny voice." Alice is "boss of the school playground" and has a "favorite torture" of her own that she learned from her brother: grabbing a classmate's hand and scraping "the back of it over the gravel-studded asphalt" ("Muffin," 80–81). This time a small girl with blonde braids replaces the immigrant boy as victim; yet Daisy is not the outsider child here; in fact, it is her popular "insider" status that Alice covets—thus her antagonism. Alice is finally routed by a kick in the shins from Daisy and a nip in the heels by a small, barking dog (Muffin).

Alice is perhaps less evil in any metaphysical sense than she is simply overbearing and cruel, in the same way that the Cornish boy Bill is merely rude and cunning and Richie Moore, certainly the product of his father's prejudice against immigrants, is both insulting and destructive. But all of these child bullies are members of the same venomous *beast* family, and Richie may be a closer "relative" of the Wiggs brothers than is readily apparent. Following the scene depicting Richie's bullying of Manny, Cooper produces a scene of a mink breaking into a chicken house, seizing the chickens by the neck, biting hard at the back of their heads, then dropping them. The mink kills for the sake of killing (rather than for food), Will's brother James has learned from a newspaper story. It kills for the *love* of killing, Will adds, implying that the dark forces may be inhabiting these animal creatures. Thus the mink produces for Will an "overwhelming awareness of evil,"[6] not unlike the paralysis Derek feels watching the Wiggs boy strangling the cat.

Peter steps in quickly to stop the torture by throwing stones at the boys (he casts the first stone, an act that leads to full-scale "war" between the two gangs). The boys of the Wiggs gang run away, and the cat is saved. But David Wiggs is labeled by Derek's gang as "beastly," a "pig," and a "Nazi" (*DF,* 38). The narrator again calls him that "weaselly Wiggs boy" (*DF,* 38), and the weasel-mink thread, denoting a wild thirst for cruelty that runs through these books, is worth noting since it seems to signal something beyond class conflict.

Although Bill, the Cornish boy, and David Wiggs represent a less fortunate economic class than the Drew children or Derek and his friends, Richie Moore's father, despite *Rich*ie's name, is decidedly middle class. Cooper appears to be saying that savagery can be found anywhere, anytime. Evil is irrational and always with us; thus to attempt to find some reason or motivation for the Wiggs brothers' behavior may be futile. Abuse of power or strength is an omnipresent human possibility that demands constant vigilance on the part of both the individual and the members of social and cultural groups.

As this day continues, Derek and his friends wander out behind his house into a thicket in a nearby field and find a place to build their camp not far from the army camp stationed in this area. They squeeze under a barbed-wire fence to find the perfect place in the wall of a ditch (an abandoned road), producing more suggestions of *Peter Rabbit,* as well as a reason why Cooper turned herself into a boy here: Flopsy, Mopsy, and Cottontail did not have the exciting adventures that Peter did. This male character is sensitive and can even be afraid at times; thus Derek makes an excellent observer of his experiences.

Thematic Focus and Narrative Voice

During an air raid that night, Derek stops to look at the sky; when his father grabs him and pushes him roughly into the shelter, Derek bursts into tears. This is his initiation; his father's violence awakens him to reality, although later he can only think about the camp and wonder if it is safe. Thus adult and child worlds are different. Cooper is showing parallel worlds—not of time, as she will later explore in the *Dark Is Rising* sequence—but of adult and child perceptions. The theme is war as it affects the child's world—children who are forced to squeeze under the barbed wire of adulthood.

When Monday finally arrives, the children return to school and discover that an old lady in the house next door has been killed when a bomb hit her home. The school has not been damaged, but classes are dismissed, so Peter brings Tom Hicks, an older boy, to see the camp. Since, at 16, he is now old enough, Tom is going into the Navy; at the camp, Tom finds a can and steps forward to fling it far out into a field.

A week passes; on Saturday the boys finish their camp. They had carved out a hole and fitted a packing case into it, producing a V-shaped room with two earthen walls formed by the side and end of the ditch. (Living through a war, they play war.) Peter debates whether he should leave his gun there. One could not buy such a "splendid long barreled metal gun" (*DF*, 82) in wartime, he knows. But the others are leaving their treasures, so he capitulates in fairness to them. After all, a soldier makes sacrifices, as Tom has taught them.

When an air raid siren sounds, they scurry home "like dutiful rabbits, over the fence, across the field and the garden, and each of them was [soon] breathless in his own house" (*DF*, 86). They are children playing at being adults; at the same time, through their play, they are also working at being children. And their camp, a haven during this time of war, helps them to fill both roles.

The next Sunday they decide to show Tom the completed camp, and on the way they meet David Wiggs and some of the White Road gang, who are chanting strange words about a kitty. When the boys arrive at their destination, there is nothing to show. The camp has been "wrecked with such savage thoroughness" (*DF*, 93), that even the outlines of the walls are scarcely visible, notes the narrator, who at times speaks through Derek's eyes and at other times speaks at some distance from him.

Derek "was looking at Peter, and he never forgot what he saw on Peter's face" *(DF,* 93), the narrator says, but this is a different narrative voice; now we hear an adult looking back at the child Derek, who has since passed into adulthood. Derek sees that Peter's gun is gone. The next voice is his child's voice again, and it is more stark and realistic in terms of unrelenting details than is usually seen in a children's book:

> The thing that Derek noticed last of all was a thing that seemed to have no meaning: a small black heap that he took to be a wet crumpled rag, lying neatly in the very center of all the mess. His eyes and mind flickered on to it, and he wondered emptily where it had come from, and then he looked away again to a small blue-flecked fragment, pathetically delicate against the trampled orange mud, that he knew was a piece of Geoffrey's blackbird's egg. He stared down at it, not daring to look at any of the others. Peter stepped down beside him, slithering a little, and put one foot out gingerly to prod the crumpled black rag; Derek watched him, still numb.
> Peter said, 'It's the cat.' (94)

Although *Dawn of Fear* was at its inception a somewhat nontraditional children's book, it has now become a more conventional one. This is because, in the last 25 years, children's books have begun depicting more death, violence, and loss of innocence than formerly. Furthermore, authors have experimented more with narrative strategies, such as the three intersecting narrative voices in *Dawn of Fear.* First, there is the omniscient narrator. (An adult is calling the world of childhood into existence in order to explain, re-create, or remember it; this involves a sorting out of the child's world or the culture of childhood.) Then there is the child's own perspective, seen in Derek's thoughts, ideas, and feelings. (The adult engages in life through the child's eyes, exploring child culture by participating in it.)

Finally there is the merging of the two in an older Derek, an adult looking back, telling about a modern human world through the children of that world. Cooper uses the lens of her own childhood to make sense of that world. The tone of this third voice permeates the fabric of the book, producing literature of child culture. But when Cooper submitted the book to publishers in the late 1960s, they were not ready for a book that did not fit easily into either the adult's or children's category. Since Margaret McElderry had by this time published *Over Sea, Under Stone* on her American list, Cooper wrote to her asking for advice. McElderry recommended that she cut some of the "adult reflective passages" ("SC" 1988, 77) and that she change the title in order to place the book more firmly on the child's list. Then she accepted it herself for publication.

The title change is significant for shifting the emphasis from adult preoccupations (the children's camp—where the cat is victimized by the dreadful Wiggs brothers—as symbol of the concentration camp) to the child's world of newly learned fears. But even when the book was finally published, reviewers were uneasy about the complexities of theme, symbol, and genre, as well as the evil of the child's world emanating from the Wiggs brothers, and reception was mixed, to say the least.

"It is a well-written, 'realistic' tale about a group of boys living on a housing estate during the Second World War," said one reviewer, "and had the author limited her horrors to death from bombs *or* to really vicious gang warfare *or* to tormenting an animal I might well have felt that this was a praiseworthy study of a serious theme which children ought to recognise. But the combination of all three seems to me phoney, gratuitously nasty and fundamentally pointless."[7] This reviewer misses the point: how Cooper links all three of these subjects in the triad of cat/victim/Nazi war crimes and the dual meaning of the word *camp*.)

Another critic felt that a "local squabble between rival gangs taking place beneath the German bombing of London," was "an interesting idea, but the conflict was poorly motivated, not deeply explored," and it descended ultimately "to the banality of mud-slinging (literally)."[8]

Emotional Resonance and Authorial Vision

The mud-slinging incident begins with Johnny Wiggs's turning up at the end of White Road on this Sunday when the cat is found dead and Tom's deciding that Johnny has had some large part in the cat's drowning. He suggests to his friends that they retaliate by wrecking the camp of the White Road boys. Derek points out the illogic of sinking to their level, and they decide on an ambush instead (mud from the ditch slung at their enemies).

The kids' version of war takes place the next Monday and Tuesday, with battle strategies, assignments of duty, transport of ammunition, waiting in the "trenches" for action to begin, and the roar of battle (the mudslinging). The counterattack is a fistfight between Tom and Johnny

Wiggs, which all of the children watch, paralyzed by fear. The war has come right into their child's play world now: the raw emotions, danger, and vengeance of adult values in conflict (responsibility versus irresponsibility), or, as Derek sees it, "the whole world had suddenly divided into two" (*DF,* 135).

Then the air raid siren erupts, the children disperse, and that night the worst possible happens. The noise of the bombing is so close and so loud that it was "as if the world had blown up" (*DF,* 142). And in a sense it has. Peter's house receives a direct hit, and no one survives, since they are all under the table in the "Morrison." The world now stops for Derek, his childhood world leveled with Peter's house. He goes to see the site where "the gateposts had held; they still stood there . . . an entrance to nowhere" (*DF,* 154). England would survive, it is implied, because of the strength and sacrifice of people like Peter, Derek, Tom and their families, but the gate swinging back and forth for easy passage in or out of childhood is standing alone.

Unlike Peter Rabbit, Peter Hutchins cannot go home at the end of this story. There is no mother serving camomile tea—no mother, no kitchen, no house. Derek is "appalled by the gate without knowing why. It was all wrong that it should be there; all wrong to be able to see it, or even open it, and not to be able to go through to everything that had always been there on the other side" (*DF,* 154). This is no traditional children's book, we may decide; such books always leave the child character with at least the illusion of innocence (Peter Rabbit returns home changed, yes, but once inside the garden gate, inside his mother's kitchen, he is as safe as any adult waking from a nightmare—evil glimpsed but innocence *restored*). Cooper leaves no escape hatch for Derek, once the cat and Peter are killed; Derek cannot go home again.

When David Wiggs returns Peter's gun, Derek buries it beside the dead cat where the camp once was. With this simple act, Peter, hero and victim, stalwart and alone, becomes fused in Derek's mind with the drowned cat. The story ends with Derek, the adult he has had to become and the child he still is, sitting in the ruins of the camp sobbing.

In the next decade, Cooper would write four books about a boy who, at 11 years of age, was born an "Old One," with immense power and insight for his meager years. But with *Dawn of Fear,* she had already set her authorial vision of the world in motion: that childhood and adulthood are not separate states, not even a continuum; children are us, as she would later say, "not yet wearing our heavy jacket of Time" (*DW,* 122).

Chapter Three

The 1970s: The *Dark Is Rising* Sequence (England)

Upon completing *Over Sea, Under Stone,* Susan Cooper knew she had grown attached to her character Merriman Lyon, and the thought crossed her mind to do something more with him later and perhaps with the Drew children, too, although she did not have definite plans to write a sequel. As she tells the story:

> About five years went by, in the space of which I married, came to America to live, wrote a couple of adult books, and had a baby. Then one snowy day I was cross-country skiing with my husband in Massachusetts, where we live . . . I was tramping along in silence, looking at the snowdrifts, seeing small trees sticking up out of the snow and thinking they looked like the antlers of deer—and then for no good reason at all, I suddenly knew that I was going to write a book, set for the most part in thick snow like this, about a small boy who woke up one birthday morning and found he was able to work magic. (*DW,* 7–8)

She jotted down her idea, wrote two more books for adults, and produced another baby (all of this in a three-year span). Then one day she happened to be rereading the part in *Over Sea, Under Stone* in which Merriman Lyon talks about the struggle of the Dark and the Light, with neither ever winning, since "there is something of each in every man" (*OSUS,* 71), and she remembered "the image of the snow and the antlered snowdrifts" (*DW,* 8). Suddenly what came into her mind was "the pattern not only of that book [*The Dark Is Rising*] but of the overall sequence of five, each dealing with different aspects of the long struggle" (*DW,* 8) that Merriman Lyon had talked about in *Over Sea, Under Stone.* "So I made an outline of each," she says, "characters and plot and setting, and before I started to write the second, *The Dark Is Rising,* I wrote the last page of the very last book" (*DW,* 8).

This last book of the sequence, *Silver on the Tree,* was published in 1977, 12 years after the first book appeared in 1965. (The second, *The*

Dark Is Rising, appeared in 1973; the third, *Greenwitch,* in 1974; and the fourth, *The Grey King,* in 1975.) *Over Sea, Under Stone* is the simplest of the books, written especially for young readers, at least as Cooper began the book. The four books written after it are more complex, and Cooper's choice of genre—legendary time fantasy—gives them an even stronger complexity. Charlotte Spivack even considers the books "mature," as opposed to juvenile, fantasy because of the complex narrative structure, the highly conceptualized scheme of time and space, and the fact that adults are featured as betrayers.[1]

In fact, since *Over Sea, Under Stone* is basically realistic fiction with certain fantasy touches woven through it (a mythic, Merlin-like, adult figure and children involved in a quest for a chalice supposedly made in the days of King Arthur), we may speak of two *Dark Is Rising* sequences, the one marketed as a group, including all five books, and the four fantasies Cooper wrote in the 1970s that begin with *The Dark Is Rising.*

The Dark Is Rising

Cooper's second book of the *Dark Is Rising* sequence is so different from the earlier work, *Over Sea, Under Stone,* that we might be tempted to call it the first of the sequence or to wish that Cooper had kept the book an independent entity, naming her Merlin character something different from Merriman Lyon, since he is now such a very different character. This Merriman is much less "in the world"; in fact, he rarely steps into the real world without quickly stepping out of it into an earlier time (there is no time-slip device in the earlier book). The style of writing, the extent of metaphysical discussion, the way the book is divided (parts here versus chapters in the earlier book), and the genre all set the book apart from its predecessor. So we begin here, in the 1970s, with a new fictional format, new characters, and a new quest, linked only very loosely to what transpired before.

Part One: "The Finding"

It is the eve of Will Stanton's 11th birthday, and Frank Dawson, who owns the farm nearby, gives him a strange present, a circular black metal (iron) ornament "quartered by two crossed lines,"[2] a Celtic symbol used well before Christianity, as Graeme Fife explains, to mean "mortal life—mortality's two intersecting lines, ringed by the unbroken circle of immortality."[3]

" 'The Walker is abroad,' " Dawson tells Will. " 'And this night will be bad, and tomorrow beyond imagining' " (*DR,* 5). But who is the Walker? Only an old tramp is lurking about when Will and his brother James are out feeding the rabbits, an old man who attracts the attention of two large rooks that come sweeping down at him, sending him rushing away in terror.

That night a snowstorm arrives, and a rook flies into the skylight of the attic room where Will sleeps, breaking the catch and leaving a heap of snow on the floor and an "empty feeling of fear" (*DR,* 15). But music wakens him the next morning, and he walks out into a "whole strange-familiar world, glistening white" (*DR,* 16), where rooks, fields, and lawns have disappeared, and only trees remain. (Actually, it is a forest of massive trees that he sees). This is a unique way for an author to send a character five centuries back in time. Having wished for snow for his birthday, Will may have unconsciously invited this time-slip, for he knows that this Midwinter Day "had been waiting for him to wake into it since the day he had been born, and, he somehow knew, for centuries before that" (*DR,* 18).

A white horse takes him off to the Chiltern Hills beyond his home in the Thames Valley of Buckinghamshire. There on a snowy hillside, he falls from the horse to find himself standing before two great wooden doors. (Prominent images in Celtic mythology for entry into the spirit world are "secret oaken doors,"[4] and Merriman will later describe them as a gateway into Time.) At this point, the doors swing open to reveal a large, windowless hall filled with strange, rich tapestries and two figures, an old lady "fragile as a bird" (*DR,* 28) and a tall man with an "arched nose fierce as a hawk's beak" (*DR,* 28).

Into this room goes Will to be instructed about who he truly is, one of those born with the gift of "high purpose" (*DR,* 31), in this case, of devoting themselves to a long conflict between Light and Dark. As the man explains, his birth some 10 years before this completed the circle of the Old Ones "that has been growing for four thousand years in every oldest part of this land. Now that Will has come into this power at age 11, his task is to make the circle "indestructible" (*DR,* 36). He must find and keep six great "Signs" of the Light, made by the Old Ones, so that they can be joined by the completed circle. Thus his name is "Sign-Seeker" (*DR,* 36), and finding the Signs is his first quest, for the Dark is Rising, the man tells Will. The old man further instructs Will, who has already seen the Dark Rider, that Will and the White horse must go to the Hunter. Meanwhile, the Walker will give him the next Sign. When he does, says this tall man, who calls himself Merriman Lyon, he will be there, too.

Suddenly the Dark is pushing at the door, barring Will's way out. And the Lady, who "in her time [has] had many, many names" (32), speaks to the Dark without words as she moves toward the doors, which then open. She alone has the power to overcome the midwinter power of the Dark—but at a price. The Lady fades away, her presence drained now from the heavy task she has just completed. She will return in time, Merriman says mysteriously.

Cooper will later, in the last book of the sequence, *Silver on the Tree,* describe the Lady as "the last height of power" (*ST,* 45) and the "queen of every hive" (*ST,* 169), words fitting two prominent figures of Celtic folklore: Guinevere of Arthurian legend and the Mother Goddess, or universal mother, of Celtic myth. Of Guinevere, Goodrich says, "We still have more names to call her by than any earthly woman who ever lived."[5] She lists 23 names, the earliest being Guinevere's priestess name, Guanhumara, included in Geoffrey of Monmouth's *History of the Kings of Britain* (c. 1135–50). A later name is that of Gwenhywyvar, from the *Mabinogian,* an early-twelfth-century collection of medieval tales of Welsh mythology. According to Goodrich, the syllable *an* in a Celtic name is related to that of the Roman god Janus, which means *passageway* and also describes individuals named as "universal mother" (Goodrich, 223).

The mother goddess, as Peter Ellis notes, was the "symbol of knowledge and freedom" and the "moral pivot of society."[6] As the Great Mother Goddess or Universal Mother, the Lady could encompass all female figures of importance in Celtic matriarchal order, reflecting the belief that one soul passes to another, according to the Celtic belief in a transmigration of souls. Or she could embody the various legends of Guinevere that have emerged in different cultural "hives," with Guinevere becoming a cultural or Celtic symbol of the Mother Goddess here (especially since Cooper will be giving her a son later in *The Grey King*). At no point in the sequence, however, does Cooper unveil the mysterious Lady, and readers are left to imagine who she is, as Will at this point might be doing as he finds himself once more near his home.

He and Merriman are approaching Huntercombe Manor (the setting of a great hall of centuries before), the place Will loves to visit in springtime when daffodils bloom. Merriman says that those of the "Circle" are "planted loosely within Time," that "all times co-exist" (*DR,* 45) for them. He has a "place" in Will's present time, he explains, but not the same one he had in *Over Sea, Under Stone*. As Will soon learns, Merriman is the butler of Huntercombe Manor, rather than a professor, as in the earlier book, and he will find Will when the next Sign is on Will's belt. A few days later, when the Walker has given Will the next circle—one of bronze—one of the Dark tries to steal it, and Merriman suddenly appears to prevent the theft.

All the time Merriman has been talking to Will, in both old time or present time, he is teaching him about the Old Ones and their magic, where "every smallest word has a weight and a meaning" (*DR,* 59). Will is learning, often the hard way, to trust his intuition (to accept his power and do his duty when the times comes) and never to do anything for spite or pride. Thus we see more of Will's gift as an Old One: the ability to transcend the thoughts and imaginings of others or connect empathetically with them. When the Walker hesitates to give Will the bronze circle, uncertain that Will is the right, the destined, one, Will understands: "He's been frightened so long, Will thought, that he's forgotten how to stop. How awful, to be so absolutely lonely. He doesn't know how to trust me; it's been so long since he trusted anyone, he's forgotten how" (*DR,* 53).

Part Two: "The Learning"

Christmas caroling takes Will to Huntercombe Manor, and Merriman turns up as Miss Greythorne's butler, but not for long. Suddenly, during the singing, time stops for everyone but Merriman and Will, who slip down the hall to the place where the tall, carved doors opened before, and once again they move into an earlier time at the Manor House (1875), when Merriman's butler attire is simply the fashion of the day for men.

The Lady of the Manor, one of the Miss Greythornes of an earlier era, shows Will the third Sign—that of wood—which she calls the Sign of Learning. It must be renewed every hundred years, she says, because it is rowan, or mountain ash, without the sturdiness of oak but with desirable qualities of its own—the ability to see, as Druids did, with far-reaching vision—needed for this Sign (learning in this case will bring prophetic vision). She finds the Sign in a log, smoldering in the ashes of her fireplace, and because she cannot give him the Sign in her own century, she places it into a hole in the wooden paneling behind a carved rose.

Then a little man in green named Hawkin draws Will through a side door into a small library with a grandfather clock. He explains to Will that the Old Ones travel in Time and are not bound by the usual rules. Will could affect history in secret ways that men would not know, he claims.

Merriman appears and explains that Hawkin comes from (or belongs in) the thirteenth century; however, by Merriman's "art," the man Hawkin has been brought forward in time for this one day. Merriman further explains that he himself belongs "nowhere and everywhere" (*DR*, 86) since he was the first Old One. He has lived in every age, and in Hawkin's age he was a Lord who reared Hawkin as his son. Hawkin, Merriman adds, will have a crucial part to play in the quest of this century, that of Will's learning about the Old Ones.

With his hand on Hawkin's shoulder, presumably to steady himself, Merriman opens the clock and pulls out what he describes as the oldest book in the world, the Book of Knowing, or "Gramarye," written in the Speech of the Old Ones, which Will understands intuitively. This will be the last day of its use: After Will reads the book, it will be destroyed forever because once he reads it, what he learns from it will never leave him. The book tells of flying, of challenge and resistance, of "Words of Power," and "of Time through the Doors" (*DR*, 91), doors standing as the way through time for the Old Ones, in any direction they choose.

But the principal way the book "tells" is through poetry and pictures that draw Will into a particular experience—"learning through feeling, feeling the way of resting on the wind . . . of sweeping and soaring" (91). The way he learns is through empathetic connection, the magical gift of the Old Ones as shaman artists, thinkers, and knowers: "And he knew as he flew that the eagle was one of the only five birds who could see the Dark, and instantly he knew the other four, and in turn he was each of them" (*DR*, 91). According to Cowan, Celtic people found omens in birds; their flight and calls indicated "the wishes of the gods and goddesses" (Cowan, 85). The flight of birds and human shape changers who flew as birds was related to the autonomy of the spiritually gifted.

Will learns about the paths of the stars in the same empathetic way, by flying among them. The book teaches him patterns of survival against ill will, spells of the sea, and the secret that "water was the one element that could in some measure defy all magic; for moving water would tolerate no magic whether for good or evil, but would wash it away as if it had never been made" (*DR*, 92). Thus he learns of the Wild Magic outside the laws of the High Magic that governs the Old Ones of the Light and Dark. He also saw the story of the Old Ones:

He saw one race after another come attacking his island country, bringing each time the malevolence of the Dark with them, wave after wave of ships rushing inexorably at the shores. Each wave of men in turn grew peaceful as it grew to know and love the land, so that the Light flourished again. But always the Dark was there, swelling and waning, gaining a new Lord of the Dark whenever a man deliberately chose to be changed into something more dread and powerful than his fellows. (*DR*, 93)

He sees the first testing of the Old Ones of the Light, who for three hundred years had fought the Dark invasion of their land. They were aided by their greatest leader, who was lost in the struggle but might one day return in spirit to help them fight once more. The desire for power fuels the strength of the Dark. And it will continue to do so until the day, as Will sees on the last page of the book, that the six Signs are joined in a circle and Arthur wakes and returns.

Merriman returns to replace the book in the clock, letting a corner of it touch the pendulum, and an explosion (the destruction of book and clock) sends them both reeling backward. He allows Will to see in a time-slip what happened to Hawkin when he realized that Merriman risked his life by removing the book from the clock. (If the Dark had ever forced Merriman, by a magical spell, to take the book from the clock for *them*, Hawkin would have been killed since Merriman's hand was on his shoulder—but the book would have been saved.) At first Hawkin had proudly agreed to be used. Later the Dark convinced him that he was simply being exploited, and he faulted Merriman for valuing the book above a man's life.

In this regard, Cooper says: "The sinister side of Merriman Lyon, and indeed all the Old Ones, is that absolute good, like absolute evil, is fanatical. As one of my characters points out, there is no room for human ambiguity. Absolute good is like a blinding light, which can be very cruel, and to that extent Merriman is not a sympathetic character" (*DR*, 192). The "flaw" in the narrative structure here, if it is to match Cooper's thinking, is that Will never sees Merriman as fanatical; thus his knowledge is not expanded by this complexity of character. Should it be? Yes, especially if this is a children's book. But, as we later see, perhaps it is not.

As quickly as it happened before, Time blinks for Will, and he is back in his own century with Merriman signaling that it is time for him to take the next Sign—the wooden circle embedded in the carved wooden rose. He also has obtained "a long lifetime of discovery and wisdom"

(*DR,* 108) from the Book of Gramarye. He knows and accepts who he is now: one who inhabits "a different time-scale from that of everyone he had ever known or loved" (*DR,* 108), and best of all, it is Christmas, surely a time free from threatening actions of the Dark. Or is it?

On Christmas Day, a late birthday/Christmas present arrives for Will from his brother Stephen, a Navy man stationed in the Caribbean. It is the giant head of a stag (a mask to be worn at Carnival time there), with branching antlers, ears of a dog, eyes of a bird, beard of a goat, and on the forehead of its human face, the Sign of the quartered circle. Then the Rider of the Dark, disguised as an acquaintance of Will's father, who calls himself Mr. Mitothin, enters the Stanton home, presumably to deliver another Christmas present but really to intimidate Will with a message spoken in the Old speech, one that only Will can understand.

Will, he says, is to tell the Old Ones that the Dark will take from them the "Things of Power" (*DR,* 118) they hope to possess (the grail, the harp, the sword, and the Signs) and that they will also break the Circle of Signs before it is ever joined. Cooper's quest pattern for these books is thus set in motion as a gigantic "chess" game of Dark and Light. One side, the Light, tries to obtain the Things of Power in order to help the world of men; the other side tries to prevent the taking of these "things" in order to gain world power or dominion.

As the Christmas service ends, the Dark besieges the church by inhabiting the bodies of a flock of rooks who storm the church doors. The Old Ones—Frank Dawson; Frank's helper, Old George; Old George's son, John Wayland Smith (who shod the white mare in the time-slip on Will's birthday); and John's wife—stand at the doors to help Will. Their courage gives him strength. He has known terror the night the rook hit his attic skylight; but now he feels an even greater fear because he has learned more about the Dark. At the same time, he has also learned how to deal with the Dark. And as the direct target of the Dark, he knows he must stand alone. So with the Old Ones close by, Will stands on the church porch, holding the three signs up before him, and the rooks are at last silenced. He has driven the Dark away.

Inside the church, the signs begin to glow, and another brightness appears on the church wall. It is the fourth Sign, a circle of stone. The first Sign, of iron, came from a Celtic Old One, Frank Dawson (High Magic). The second one, of bronze, was carried by an ordinary human shaman, the Walker (human effort). The third, of wood, came from a house, Huntercombe Manor (nature). This fourth one of stone emerges from the church wall (culture). Farmer Dawson says, " 'We have the fourth Sign' " (*DR,* 129)—*we,* not *you;* thus he indicates that the power of the Light does not come from one individual or any one member of the Circle of Light but from the cohesion of the social *group.*

These signs are understood more completely if we know that Cooper in her teen years had come upon Jacquetta Hawkes's *The Land,* which became one of her favorite books (later Hawkes and her husband, J. B. Priestley, became close friends of Cooper). In reading Hawkes's book, especially chapter 8, "Land and People,"[7] we can see Cooper's utilizing Hawkes's text to describe the land and people of England as it evolved, as symbolized by the "Signs"—Bronze, Iron, Wood, Stone, Gold (fire), and Water. There were the Bronze and Iron ages, the growth of forests (wood), the Avebury and Stonehenge projects, the prehistoric prospecting for gold and the forging of ornaments, weapons, and tools, and the water bringing Neolithic people across the English Channel as invaders and settlers.

Finally on this Christmas Day, one of the rooks beckons to Will. Around the corner of the churchyard, Will discovers the Walker asleep in the snow. Will and his brother Paul take the old tramp home with them, hoping to save his life, for a blizzard is quickly encircling London, shutting down power and transportation, more malevolence of the Dark. Deep in the night, Merriman appears to confirm his feelings: The Dark is at its most powerful at this time of the Christmas festival of 12 days and nights. He says: " 'Theirs is a cold strength, the winter feeds it. They mean to break the Circle forever . . . But not all things go according to their will. Much magic still flows untapped along the Old Ones' ways. And we may find more hope in a moment' " (*DR,* 136–37).

Out the window they fly on a broad ribbon-road, in a "bubble of Time" to a "ghostly grove of trees" (*DR,* 137), where a procession of pipe and drum players marches past—the yearly ritual of the Hunting of the Wren. Says Fife, "The wren is the spirit of the Old Year killed at the Winter Solstice" [155], and the ancient Celts celebrated this belief by hunting the wren on St. Stephen's feast day, December 26, and killing it with stones.

Instead of the wren in the woven branches, they see the Lady lying there "delicate as a bird" (*DR,* 138). The players stop before Will with three messages: he should beware the snow, the Dark is rising, and the Lady will return. They chant the same poem Merriman chanted earlier in the great hall of the Chiltern Hills, plus another announcing, in a brief verse, where the last two Signs will be found, in "Fire in the candlering," and "water from the thaw":

The third [boy], in a quick sing-song tone, chanted something that Will recognized as soon as it began:

> 'When the Dark comes rising . . .
> Iron from the birthday, bronze carried long;
> Wood from the burning, stone out of song;
> Fire in the candle-ring, water from the thaw;
> Six signs the circle, and the grail gone before.' (*DR*, 38)

The Celtic poet was a "master of spiritual innuendo and mind-stretching allusions," says Cowan:

> A popular Welsh literary form, the *gnome*, is a brief, almost haikulike verse that juxtaposes images . . . The impact of these poems comes not from making a rational connection between the apparently unrelated images, but letting the mystery of their union work its subtle influence over the imagination. If they leave the listener feeling unsettled and intellectually unsatisfied, it is because their meaning is not meant to be fully comprehended on the first encounter. Like the [Zen] koan with its inscrutability and the haiku with its disarming simplicity, the full significance of the gnome may come only gradually, if at all. (102)

Cooper uses this gnome verse form to link this book to the next titles in the sequence and also to help the child characters puzzle out the mystery of their quest; we will see its special use emerging later in *The Grey King*. Here the pipe and drum players are practicing the ancient art of augury when they make their verse-chant prophecies about the Lady and the Signs. Significantly, the Lady is associated with the wren, who, Ellis notes, is "a bird of augury among the Britons."[8] In a later book she tells Jane how the children will find the last "Thing of Power"; thus she functions as soothsayer, prophet, and master of the art of augury.

At this point Merriman disappears, with a warning to Will to " 'be wary of the snow' " (*DR*, 139), and Will falls back to sleep with the word "beware" ringing in his ears.

Part Three: "The Testing"

First Will has learned who he is (one of the Old Ones, the youngest and last of them, who will find the Signs and close the Circle against the Dark for all time); then he has learned how to be what he is (he is trained as an Old One by the Book of Gramarye). Now he is to be tested—left virtually alone to do what has been asked of him. The word *virtual* is important here since it is not until the penultimate book of this sequence that Will is left really alone to work through his quest. Here he is simply taking the first step—and walking a bit shakily. His missteps are meant to reveal the transition from the boy who is learning to accept his power to the Old One who passes the test.

With news that the storm is worsening, Will sets out for groceries and meets Merriman, who announces to the villagers that Miss Greythorne is opening up the manor as an emergency shelter for all. He tells Will to move the Walker to the Manor as quickly as possible since the Dark Rider poses a danger to him and his family. On arriving at the Manor, Merriman tells Hawkin there is still time for him to rejoin the Light. But Hawkin is too filled with resentment to do so. Merriman, he charges, risked his life for a book.

Hawkin either misses the point about the book's importance to the quest or about the quest itself or he is making the point that no one's life is worth risking regardless of the "greater good" (isolationist policy in times of military aggression, such as the Nazi invasion of European countries in the late 1930s). When Hawkin complains about the burden of carrying the Sign for so many centuries and about being unable to die as mortal men do, Will feels the pain of Hawkin's life, and it becomes apparent that Hawkin is the Walker in an earlier time.

The Walker is aptly named in Celtic terms. Shamanism, says Cowan, quoting Joseph Campbell in *The Way of the Animal Powers,* calls a man or woman to become a " 'walker between the worlds' of ordinary and nonordinary reality" (Cowan, 11). It was several chapters into the book, Cooper says, when "bright-eyed young Hawkin turned up and I realized that he and the Walker were going to be one and the same man."[9] But linking the one that she has described as a "shambling old man" ("HWV," 30) and the other, in her words "a kind of Everyman figure, hopeful, fallible, and eventually doomed" ("HWV," 30), certainly fuses ordinary and nonordinary reality in a powerful human metaphor.

When the Walker's raving becomes incessant, the doctor gives him an injection. With the subduing of the Walker, the next Sign (Fire) emerges. Carrying the candles of modern time to the nine empty sockets of past time, the Old Ones produce, in the Lady's Hall, a "triumphant circle of fire" (*DR,* 170). The Lady explains that the candles, used by the Dark for destructive purposes, will now be used for bringing in the Sign of Fire; the last candle that is put in place (the one Will brought) now blazes high into the mandala of a golden flower. When the petals melt way, the seedpod breaks open, revealing a small golden cross-quartered circle.

According to Jung and Jaffe, such a "magic circle" or mandala symbolizes the "psychic totality"[10] of the centered self. It appears in the form of a flower (as Cooper shows here), a wheel (as it will later appear in *Silver on the Tree*), a cross, and a circle divided into four (as we see in the cross-quartered signs Will is collecting throughout this book). According to Jung, mandalas appear during times of chaos and confusion to provide order or to hold things together, just as the circle of Old Ones is attempting to quell the Dark and bring about world order.

Then the rain begins and with it the most dangerous time of the Dark—that of Twelfth Night. Will discovers that his mother has fallen and may have broken her leg and that his sister Mary is missing. The Dark, Merriman has just warned Will, cannot harm or destroy humans. But they can lead men to harm themselves. " 'They can encourage men's own instincts to do them harm' " (*DR,* 172). And this is just what, in Mary's case, has happened, when she rushed impetuously out into the storm to find her brothers.

Paul and Will leave to rescue Mary, but the rooks drive the brothers off in two directions. The rain pours down, the thawing of the snow is coming, and Old George arrives. He instructs Will that the white horse must go to the Hunter and that Will must take the horse there. Old George also reminds him that " 'moving water is free of magic' " (*DR,* 179). It will take sides with neither the Dark nor the Light.

When Will soon sees the horned carnival head floating in the stream (the flood having carried it out of his house), he remembers that in water, the Dark cannot use the head to its own ends. He reflects on the Thames as one of the "ancient things from the beginning of Time" (*DR,* 182). There are the Things of *nature,* or the "Wild Magic," of which the Signs are made, and there are the Things of Power, of *culture,* or what those of the Light or Dark did with the ancient things: They shaped them into ornaments. (According to Celtic belief, gods were everywhere, especially in trees and water. Rivers were thought to be possessed of spirits and "regarded as a numinous life-force."[11] Rivers such as the Thames received offerings of weapons, shields, and, as we see here, a carnival mask that Herne the Hunter will eventually find and wear as his armor.)

From a piece of high ground, Will climbs down and begins to explore. He encounters Hawkin, who tells him that Mary is now a hostage of the Dark and that Will should offer Mary in exchange for the Signs. Should he risk Mary's life or save it? He thinks of Mary and worries that because of him, her life is at stake. Then a voice that he recognizes as Merriman's sounds in his mind, reminding him that he serves a larger cause—keeping the Dark from rising. Placing his trust in Merriman to see Mary through this "play" in the game, he refuses to give up the Signs, calling the Dark Rider's bluff. Suddenly "happy witless Mary" (*DR,* 188) appears before him, seated on the Rider's horse. He calls for the Light, and Merriman arrives on the white mare to carry her off to safety. (When you find yourself in the grip of fear or mind games played by the Dark, those of the Light will support you if you simply trust them to do so, Will sees.)

At this moment, the prow of a ship appears on the Thames, carrying the body of a dead king of the "Dark" Ages, in whose cold hands Will sees the last Sign. This time it is made of glass (the Sign of Water). Merriman returns to tell Will to take the Sign, explaining that the Dark lost its hold on Mary because the Sign of Water is one of the oldest and most powerful signs. Thus the Signs can now be united against the Dark for all time. A larger good (collecting the last and most powerful Sign) achieves the smaller good—Mary's safety in the snowstorm. But all is far from over. Will glimpses in the distance a tornado of the Dark forces approaching. The Signs are not yet joined (the last task). " 'If the Dark can take you now,' Merriman tells Will, 'they take all that they need to rise to power. Now they will try hardest of all' " (*DR,* 194).

The metaphor is again that of the chess board, and the question arises, Is there more to Cooper's pattern here than mere game playing, the suspense and excitement of the Light "players" defeating the Dark? What does this quest of the Old Ones, with Will as central player, signify? There is, of course, the human need, particularly the child's, to "translate" the world or shape meaning about the world from text. Will succeeds through courage, trust, intuition, imagination, and empathy, or what Cooper will later describe as "fierce caring" (*ST,* 272). But beyond the *how,* there is the *why.* Because human voices wake us (Hawkin's tragedy is one that we cannot take lightly), we learn that we are an important part of a larger pattern, one that imposes heavy burdens. And when the time comes, we either accept those burdens or collapse, as Hawkin does, under their weight.

Because Will has played his part well this night, when Herne the Hunter rides the Wild Hunt, as he does every Twelfth Night, " 'the Hunt will have a quarry' " (*DR,* 195), Merriman says. It will rout the Dark so that the Signs can be joined, the last task of this particular quest. When the carnival head appears, borne by the river, it is Will's next task to take it to Herne the Hunter, who now sits astride the white mare.

(Herne is the Anglo-Celtic name of Cernunnos, the Great Horned God of European lore, who appears in paintings and sculpture wearing horns of the ram and antlers of the stag. Master of the hunt, he "came into his full power in late summer and early fall; thus here we see him in late winter or early spring in all his regenerative power, from the cyclical shedding of his antlers."[12])

The hunter takes the mask, and, when he puts it on, the two heads, his own and that of the mask, become one (the mask becomes real). Will sees the man's eyes as the "strange tawny eyes" (*DR,* 198) of a bird with the "fierce inevitability of nature" (*DR,* 199). The Light is as cold as the Dark at times because winning is as important for their cause as it is for the Dark's.

In the Wild Hunt that ensues (in Celtic legend, the "Wild" or "Divine" Hunt signifies a rounding up of souls to take to the Underworld, and Herne is a death deity, according to McCoy), the Dark is lashed to its destruction—at least for the moment—and its Lords must wait for their next chance, Merriman explains. But once the Six Signs are joined, the Light will be much stronger. For Will, it is back to John Wayland Smith, a figure of German myth possessing sword-making arts, and his smithy. The joining is done in a " 'bubble of time' " (*DR,* 205) between Smith's century and Will's because the signs were collected in Will's time, when the smithy was no longer there.

The joining is celebrated by the Old Ones, who arrive from places all around the world and from all times. "These are my people," Will says to himself, "linked for the greatest purpose in the World" (*DR,* 206). The Lady arrives once more on the bier of the wren, but this time she steps down to officiate at the ceremony. The Signs, she explains, are one of the four " 'Things of Power that have slept these many centuries, and they are a great part of our strength' " (*DR,* 208). Each was made in a different time by a different craftsman working for the Light, she explains. There is the grail, the Circle of Signs, a golden harp, and a crystal sword. The harp and the sword are still to be retrieved from other times and places where they lie "sleeping."

For now, she adds, Will has completed a great quest and proved himself strong. He has become part of a pattern larger than he, but he has also learned—and revealed, when he trusted Mary to Merriman's care— that anyone in the pattern still has free *will,* just as Hawkin does. (Humans and Old Ones both have choices, and it is wisdom, courage, trust, and responsibility that guide these choices.) When Merriman explains that Hawkin could always have chosen to die as a human,

Hawkin at last chooses death, making his peace with the Light as he goes.

It is time to go home now, Merriman tells Will. In parting, he gives Will a gift from Miss Greythorne, a small hunting horn that we will see again in this sequence, but not for a while. For the moment, Will returns to being just a boy in his own time, as Merriman turns into the "tall carved doors" that lead "out of Time" (*DR,* 216).

Thus ends *The Dark Is Rising,* a mythic fantasy with a child protagonist, a very unusual genre blending that resulted in the book's being marketed for children, since in this cultural era, adult and child characters are segregated in books and on bookshelves. (Thus adults at times miss the best books.) Or perhaps we live in an era when adults feel that children's literature is unrelated to their own lives. Just as children's literature was once perceived as a moral construct, we have grown to view it as a social construct, but Cooper causes us to see it with new eyes, as an artistic construction—or simply as *literature.*

Will learns who he is at the beginning, and his quest becomes that of accepting who and what he is in order to serve that gift. This is neither an adult's nor a child's role, preoccupation, or situation. It is simply Will's blessing—or burden—in this setting and one that a reader of any age can observe with fascination and experience with pleasure. Whether children can penetrate the depths of Hawkin's story is another matter, and certainly Will, at age 11, is only beginning to understand Hawkin. Only in years to come will he be able to sort out what the 11-year-old boy barely comprehends.

It is a very different Will that we meet in the next book of the sequence, *Greenwitch.* By this time, he has grown more fully into his role (he has accepted it), and he carries the burdens of power like the Old One he truly is. His self-assurance, in fact, causes problems in the new quest adventure, since the Drew children now rejoin the cast; unfortunately, Will, who seems to know a little too much, is at the outset very much out of sync with the other children. *Greenwitch* is much more easily seen as a children's book because of this *group* of children that takes over as protagonists. But it would be a mistake to categorize the book as children's literature on the basis of protagonist alone.

Any one of the four books following *Over Sea, Under Stone* must be considered literature of dual audience, a genre of enormous potential but one that very few writers explore. The quest-fantasy form places the books outside the realm of either children's or adult literature; at the same time it encompasses them both. Because of the meaning of the quest itself, the preoccupations of children and adults become so closely intertwined that they cannot be considered separately. The fate of *human* life is the subject here, as it is in other quest fantasies of dual audience, like Virginia Hamilton's *Justice* trilogy and Alan Garner's *Stone Book* quartet.

Greenwitch

Composed of 13 chapters (as is the first book, *Over Sea, Under Stone*), Susan Cooper's next book of the sequence is not arranged in parts as with the book preceding it and the ones following it. *Greenwitch* really forms the sequel to *Over Sea, Under Stone* rather than to *The Dark Is Rising*. Like *Over Sea, Under Stone,* which is also set in southern Cornwall, in the far west region of England, this book moves through a series of seven, highly charged, dramatic scenes or scene-clusters: the making of the Greenwitch, Jane in the sea, the caravan, Tethys's world, the Greenwitch on the quay, Jane and the Greenwitch, and recapturing the grail.

The Making of the Greenwitch

Simon, Jane, and Barney stand before an empty glass case in the British Museum. The grail they discovered the previous summer in a cove in Cornwall has now been stolen. The children are understandably dejected that after all their hard work delivering the grail to safety, in the face of the "horrible Mr. Hastings" (*G,* 2),[13] they have been foiled. And worse, there is no one they can tell about Hastings. Who would believe them? Hastings is a shape changer with power to become different people in different times and places (a shaman figure working for the Dark).

Fortunately, at this moment, Great-Uncle Merry appears, the theft having drawn him back from an Oxford sabbatical in Greece. Merry knows that some agent of the Dark has taken the grail, as he says, " 'to help them on the way to something else' " (*G,* 4), but he does not tell them what, only that if they are to help in this new quest to retrieve the stolen grail, they must be willing to do so largely on the basis of trust. They agree. They know Merry to be mysterious, but it is mystery for a good cause—or even the best: "[T]he long struggle for control of the world between the Light and the Dark" (*G,* 6). And the grail is one of the objects of power that will help unravel the quest. So the children are soon on a train again, bound for a week at the little seaside town of Trewissick.

Enter Will Stanton, that also enigmatic but very humanlike boy, from *The Dark Is Rising,* the youngest of the Old Ones, Guardians of the Light, who became aware of his destiny only very recently, when the Dark was once again rising. It is springtime and Will has a vacation from school. His Uncle Bill, who has come from America to visit pottery factories in the area, invites Will to accompany him and a friend to Cornwall on a business trip. When the friend turns out to be Merriman, Will knows he is embarking on something other than a mere spring holiday. A pottery factory is a particularly apt choice for his uncle's "quest"; Geoffrey of Monmouth proclaimed Tintagel in Cornwall as Arthur's presumed birthplace, and in the 1930s, the Radford excavation unearthed pottery dating from the sixth century (the Arthurian period of England).[14]

The Drew children and Will settle in together uneasily. Cooper is breaking an important literary convention here in mixing characters from different books that vary in genre, setting, literary style, and artistic strength. The characters seem almost to *feel* the literary "earthquake," so disgruntled are they with one another. But this experiment produces for Merriman a reason to give some important advice: " 'Never dismiss anyone's value until you know him' " (*G,* 18), he replies when Barney describes Will as a "nuisance" (*G,* 18).

As it unfolds by the end of this sequence of books, Cooper's worldview, in terms of the mission the children undertake, requires not simply Old Ones filled with the High Magic (like Will) but also mortal children (like the Drews) to assume the legacy and responsibility that completing the quest involves. So the human children have to be involved from the beginning. Moreover, they must be working for the same goals of the Light that Will is in order to gain the intuitive knowledge of good and evil needed to turn the world in a different direction, after the last battles are won.

At the beginning, however, the children—including Will—have no idea how the quest will develop (or how one quest will generate the next). They are also unaware that they will become good friends, highly dependent on one another's different strategies and abilities as individuals with a common charge. Nor do they now see that another child will ultimately join them, one whose destiny is intertwined with theirs from the beginning and for whom their presence, particularly as *children,* is crucial to the success of the search. All they know now is what all children feel about a new kid on the block.

There are the usual rivalries for Uncle Merry's attention. Who is this intruder, Simon and Barney wonder, and how will they get on with the quest with him tagging along? Jane, always sensitive to the feelings of others, says they can at least be polite. Will is simply uneasy since he quickly senses so much more, such as that the Dark has not stolen the grail at this time, in April, for just any reason.

It is spring, the time of the Celtic festival of Beltane (Bright or Goodly-Fire), the feast that welcomed summer heat for ripening crops with bonfires to encourage the sun's appearance (Green, 55). Thus, in a mythic invention of Cooper's own, it is time for the making of the Greenwitch, something the Drew children know nothing about. They are quickly initiated when Jane, as the only female child, is invited to participate in the "making" of this figure, an "old spring rite," as Merriman explains, " 'celebrated here, for greeting summer and having a good harvest of crops and fish' " (*G,* 19). Only the women are invited to the bonfire, high on Kemare Head, to make the Greenwitch, a ceremony that takes the entire night. They do so by weaving together boughs and blossoms of the hawthorne tree for the witch's body, which is placed on a framework of hazel branches and topped with rowan leaves and branches for the witch's head. (According to Fife, the hazel tree signifies poetic wisdom [125], and Ellis [1994] cites the rowan as producing prophetic visions.)

To Jane the finished "person" is intimidating, if not frightening, more an "it" than a "she" (more a stone or tree than a person), and the fact that the women treat this object so lightly is surprising and puzzling to her: "For she knew suddenly, out there in the cold dawn, that this silent image somehow held within it more power than she had ever sensed before in any creature or thing. Thunder and storms and earthquakes were there, and all the force of the earth and sea. It was outside Time, boundless, ageless, beyond any line drawn between good and evil" (*G,* 29–30).

Great power such as this suggests to her "endless loneliness," for it was held "only in great isolation" (*G,* 30). Consequently, she feels awe and pity for this creature. The women tell her of the old saying "that whoever touches the Greenwitch before it be put to cliff and makes a wish, shall have that wish" (*G,* 104). When she is invited to join the tradition, she does not wish anything for herself such as the other girls are doing (wishing for rich husbands or for one boy in particular). She thinks of the "great loneliness" that such an "unimaginable force" (*G,* 30) seems to reveal; then she grasps one of the hawthorn branches and speaks directly to the creature, saying, " 'I wish you could be happy' " (*G,* 31).

She chides herself for what she feels is a childish wish, of placing feelings above reason (she could have wished for the grail's return). The "hard-eyed Cornishwoman" (*G,* 31) who is the leader of the "making" comments on Jane's wish, noticing the peril it involves, since what makes one person happy may incur harm or hurt to others. But good *may* come of the wish, she adds.

A great deal does come of it, in fact: without Jane's empathetic connectiveness, the quest might never have proceeded any further. But at this time Jane does not see that; she simply feels silly. There is little time to dwell on wishes, however, silly or not. Soon the harbor comes to life, with fishermen returning from their night on the water, shopkeepers, factory men, all the men of the village greeting the women. The Greenwitch is now ready to be put "to cliff' (*G,* 32) for luck in the coming year. It is the men's turn to take part in the "making." They heave the figure forward into the sea (males and females working together equally for human survival in this ancient ritual).

Cooper's Greenwitch seems to be created as a feminine principle or precursor to the more familiar Green Man, a vegetation god or tree spirit called Jack in the Green in Celtic folk tradition and, in medieval romance, the Green Knight, as Anderson notes.[15] Green Women, although rare, are known as vegetation goddesses that appear in springtime fertility ceremonies. That Cooper couples her own Green Woman with the witch figure is particularly inventive. As Ellis notes, there is no such thing as a witch in Celtic folklore, although female Druids in stories were reduced to "witch-like figures"[16] who could perform magic and produce enchantments. The witch figure in pagan thought, Murray tells us, arose from the priestess figure whose magic arts became feared and stigmatized,[17] as Jane seems to sense when she regards the figure as lonely and isolated.

While Jane is engaged in the witch making, Barney is having adventures of his own. The day before, he watches an artist making what he thinks is an ugly abstract painting because of its "particularly nasty shade, a yellowy, mustard-like green" that is *"all wrong"* (*G,* 20) for the picture. The artist becomes particularly testy when Barney asks, " 'Why not blue? Or a *better* kind of green?' " (*G,* 20). At this point, Barney begins his own picture, a sketch of the harbor, and when he has finished, the angry artist grabs the picture and runs away with it. Will suddenly appears and says the man has driven off with a dog that Barney knows is Rufus, the dog owned by Captain Toms, their landlord of the previous summer.

Jane in the Sea

At Captain Toms's home, the Grey House, where the children stayed the summer before, Merriman, Will, and the Captain try to decide whether the painter is a greater or lesser lord of the Dark. Jane, always the empathetic connector, thinks of the poor Greenwitch, alone in the deep water and hopes that the waves have not smashed it "all to bits" (*G,* 43). That night, at the height of a storm, in her great caring and concern for the Greenwitch, Jane finds herself on Kemare Head once more, where she suddenly leaps and then falls or dives into the deep water.

There she sees the Greenwitch, unchanged but alive now (with an actual face) and speaking about a secret, a "bright shining thing" that looks to Jane like "a small glowing stick" (*G,* 45). The witch guards the secret, she tells Jane. Then, fearful that Jane will reveal her secret, the Greenwitch begins to unfold her branches and grasp at Jane. Terrified, Jane promises not to tell. "Waking" to find Merriman at her bedside, she tells him about her encounter with the Greenwitch, which she interprets as a dream. Then when she is almost asleep once more, she realizes that she knows what "the small bright object" (*G,* 47) is but dozes off to sleep before she is able to remember.

Adults often interpret Jane's flight or leap into the sea as a dream. However, placed as it is before the scene in which she tells Merriman about this encounter, it appears to be neither "real" in the sense of Merry's own magical flights nor a dream, as she herself believes it to be. Rather, it seems to be something in between, such as a journey of the imagination that enables her to participate in the shaman shape-changing abilities of the Old Ones. As Cowan says, modern Celtic stories are filled with people endowed with the spirit and power "to break through ordinary consciousness" (9). These people, although untrained as shamans, manage to find their way into the mythic spirit world, where they undergo adventures like those of any other shaman-traveler.

The Caravan

Simon and Barney awaken on a perfect day for a walk. Rufus follows, showing them he wants to take them to the place where the painter took him. Up over the village, the dog takes them inland to a sign that reads PENTREATH FARM. But instead of a farm, they discover an old-fashioned gypsy caravan, bright colored and richly decorated.

The painter appears to guide them inside where they discover the ceiling of the van is painted in the same strange, disturbing colors that

Barney noticed when he watched the man working on the quay. The painter is temporarily inhabiting a gypsy caravan and assuming a gypsy identity (he has disguised himself as an artist and fortune-teller) in order to carry out his work for the Dark. He offers them orange soda, which Simon only pretends to drink. Then he directs them to a box that he takes from a cupboard, and inside the box is the stolen grail. The painter pours water into the grail, then directs Barney to look into it and tell what he sees in the water.

What happens to Barney next results from a potion in the drink; suddenly he begins receiving signs and messages from the magic liquid, but he neither knows rationally nor remembers what happens to him next. As Simon later tells the others, the voice of the water told the painter that the Greenwitch has what he seeks (the small lead case containing the second manuscript, which was lost in the sea on the day that the children found the grail—and the same "small glowing stick" that the Greenwitch showed Jane the night before). The voice tells them that the little lead case is " '[i]n the *realm of Tethys,* in the green depths *out of reach*' " (*G,* 65). The voice also tells him what spell will evoke the Greenwitch and how quickly all must be done, since the Greenwitch will soon be going to the deeper waters of Tethys.

In Tethys's World

Before the children's eyes, Will and Merriman, the shaman Old Ones, fly into the air as birds and plunge into the sea below. But when the children cry out in horror at this dangerous and "impossible" act, Captain Toms casts a spell over them, causing them to forget what they have seen. As terror drains from their faces, he directs them back to his home where they can wait and see what happens next.

Up to this point, the action of the book has moved through three of the seven dramatic scenes: the making of the Greenwitch, Jane's leap into the sea, and the scrying in the Caravan. Now, as the centerpiece of the book, Will and Merriman, in the world of the sea, encounter Tethys, the Lady of the Sea or the White Lady, as the fishermen call her. ("Tethys" is the name of a narrow sea, west of Scandinavia, running beside Scotland and Ireland in the Ordovician Age, when England was under the ocean, as Jacquetta Hawkes reveals in *The Land*.) This scene is particularly important for revealing how Cooper's quest pattern works and how the divisions of High Magic, Wild Magic, and the human world are intertwined in this particular worldview.

This "region of fear and treachery, where every fish ate every other fish" (*G,* 70) is older than the High Magic of the Old Ones and older than the world of men. Where the Wild Magic reigns, Tethys rules alone outside the High Magic, but even she still obeys certain rules: She cannot help the Light or the Dark (she has no enemies, no friends among these forces; she is neutral, seeing all but taking no side). Merriman seems to have something of a personal relationship with her, however. He flatters her (at rather lengthy intervals), and she concedes a little in return.

Merriman, it seems, had been in these depths some 15 centuries before (accompanied by another greater than himself, as she remembers) to request a favor. She had apparently provided some small help to them, although we are not told at this time what it was or that it was Arthur who accompanied him. So this time, Tethys gives them a little leeway, too: before the Greenwitch comes into this realm, she says, they may, in the name of Tethys, try to influence the Greenwitch to do what they want—give up what she has found in the sea (the bright object that Jane has seen in her dream).

Greenwitch on the Quay

At this moment, as Jane and Simon cross the quay from the cottage on the left side, facing the sea, to the Grey House on the opposite side, they spy the painter sitting at his easel. As the night wears on, even into the darkness, they take turns at Captain Toms's telescope watching the painter. Meanwhile, the Captain tells them the story of a smuggling ship, *The Lottery,* famous some two hundred years before in Cornwall and of a traitor to the town who has now become their great shame. (Smuggling was prevalent in Cornwall in the eighteenth and nineteenth centuries, because of the jagged coastline, which provided easy concealment of small craft and illicit cargo.) He tells a story of the last rising of the dark in Cornwall, how it came from the sea but was driven back by the Light. Then the "Lady" (Tethys) sent a west wind that turned it back to shore, where it was finally defeated (Tethys's favor to Merriman and Arthur).

When Captain Toms decides to go down to the harbor, the children join him. What they discover is the painter working by a light emanating from the painting itself. He is painting the spells that the voice of the scrying revealed to Barney, and they are taking effect. A gale is rising, along with the smells of foam, fish, sand, and seaweed, as the Greenwitch looms over the painter, much larger, Jane notices, than "the image of leaves and branches that she had seen earlier cast down into the sea" (*G,* 87).

The magic that produced the Greenwitch came from three kinds of plants (rowan, hazel, and hawthorne) and from the humans, female and male, who were working together for a cause—"a good harvest of crops and fish" (*G,* 19). Now the painter uses the spells of Mana, Reck, and Lire to bring the Greenwitch back out of the sea. (He funnels the magic into a much stronger channel of power.)

But Greenwitch, no matter how tall she rises, is still virtually a child. "Child of Tethys," she is called, "child of Poseidon, child of Neptune" (*G,* 88), a child still in need of guidance. And Tethys, her mother, has shown her that the painter wants the "thing of Power" (*G,* 89) she has found as a way to impress his masters. (It is his ambition to become a Great Lord of the Dark.) But when the Greenwitch turns down his request and he attempts to command her obedience, she (or her channel of powerful winds) grows larger and louder and more rebellious. Jane, because of her strong empathy, hears the witch cry out to be left alone, words the painter in his great greed and selfishness can never hear. He continues to paint the spells, eventually bringing on the unleashed power of the Wild Magic, a brilliant, dangerous green light that spreads over the village.

"All the power of the Wild Magic, which is without discipline or pattern, is let loose tonight—in this place" (*G,* 93), Merriman tells Jane before he and Will set out for the harbor. Jane watches from her bedroom window, wondering who Will really is, with his "cheerful round face" and his "blue-grey eyes" (*G,* 97). The lights of a ship take her into two time-slips. First, she experiences the initial rising of the Dark, when red-haired men in helmets (the Danes) poured into the harbor, setting Trewissick harbor and the countryside on fire. Later she sees a phantom ship, passing right over the harbor and the hills of Trewissick and out onto the moors beyond. (The phantom ship is a famous image in old Cornish legends.) Finally she sleeps, as, down below in the harbor, Merriman and Will invoke the Greenwitch, trying for themselves to obtain the shining case. Men's power struggles have nothing to do with her, the Greenwitch protests. The light, the dark, they are all self-serving, but no one cares, she cries.

Merriman prods her gently to try to remember whether anyone has ever cared. And she does remember one. The child, she says, and Will wonders for just a moment if she means him. Then she goes on (teaching him a subtle lesson about the value of females) to tell the story of Jane, who could have wished for anything, including this Thing of

Power, the night of the Greenwitch's "making," but who did not. " 'She looked at me as if I were human,' " (*G,* 104) says the Greenwitch. Remembering Jane's treatment of her as human causes the Greenwitch to become for the moment gentler, more humanlike, more reasonable.

The painter reappears to reassert his arrogant commands, and the mood of the Greenwitch changes back to anger. Then the phantom ship returns to drag the painter out of sight as it sails out to sea, leaving the Old Ones alone on the quay.

Jane and the Greenwitch

In Jane's waking "sleep" this night, she sees the Greenwitch, who explains to her what is happening: the Wild Magic is bringing back all the old troubles the town has lived through with the traitor, but the painter has been taken out of Time and will not return, the "hopeless fate," Merriman later explains, that lies waiting for any "lone figure" (*G,* 118) embarking on a quest. (We see that it takes many different kinds of beings in many different ages and places working together to produce something good.)

Jane explains to the Greenwitch how important the object is to everyone, especially those of the Light. And when the Greenwitch discovers the object is important to Jane, the one she remembers making a wish for *her,* she willingly gives up the case. Courteous, thoughtful, unselfish Jane has won this quest for them.

The next morning when she awakens, Jane finds that she is holding the little lead case. She did not do anything, she says, rushing down to tell the others; it just appeared. Will feels otherwise. She made a wish, he says. In other words, violent actions—those often relegated to males in stories and life—do not really bring about the important results human seek. It is instead emotions that do so; kindness, caring, courtesy, and unselfishness supersede actions and become actions in themselves—in this case, the most crucial actions possible.

Jane wishes that the Greenwitch could be happy; later she hopes the Greenwitch has not been destroyed by the waves (is still "alive" to be happy). Then still later, she takes action: She cares deeply, and her fierce caring takes her back to Kemare Head and down into the sea to do something about her wish. Wishing may be a preoccupation (sometimes the only solution) for females in traditional stories. But as real females know, what makes wishes come true is what they themselves do or say to bring a wish to pass.

The influence of Cooper's wide reading is evident if we remember the medieval legend of the Grail Knight who must ask the Grail King the compassionate question, What ails thee, before the king can be healed. Parzival, however, must search out the castle twice before he gains the courage to ask the question—and perhaps appear foolish for asking questions—and thus to heal the king. Jane knows intuitively to make her compassionate wish; she does not hesitate or hold back what seems to her the natural, the only, thing to say. As Lloyd Alexander says of Nesbit's wisdom and wit in *Five Children and It:* "[I]t tells us that our deepest wishes come true only by our own intelligence and our own efforts."[18]

This night Jane sets in motion a chain of events that results in her standing, at the end of the book, once more on Kemare Head, saying goodbye to the Greenwitch. Jane is the closest mortal child to an Old One in her strong, empathetic gifts, so close, in fact, that she has made a magical leap of her own into the sea, just as Will and Merriman did; hers, however, was the more successful in terms of the outcome of the quest and the personal growth she achieved. As she walks along the rocks of Kemare Head, she winces a little "as her bare feet, not yet toughened by summer, pressed against rough rock" (*G,* 128). But pressed against the rough vision of the world she has seen in this quest, Jane is a lot tougher than before. This was her quest (Cooper dedicated *Greenwitch* to her daughter Kate), and we find ourselves saying, "Well done."

Recapturing the Grail

The book winds to a close with Barney's retrieving the grail from the cupboard in the old, deserted caravan, now seen in a different "light" as dilapidated, unused for years, and no longer under the painter's spell. The three Old Ones (Merriman, Will, and Captain Toms) study the grail and manuscript side by side and decipher the hidden message that was written to save men. A poem of six lines produces a pattern of meaning they must remember, since the parchment crumbles quickly, nearly as soon as it is read. (Ancient Celts, says Simon James, "passed their wisdom from one generation to the next in the form of memorized verse, so their secrets have ultimately died with them."[19])

The words, written in Welsh, indicate, as Will sees, that the last part of the quest will take part in Wales. The setting of the *Dark Is Rising* sequence shifts to the land north of Cornwall, with the importance of Arthurian legend coming more sharply into focus as the way Cooper will illuminate her theme and vision of the world.

Chapter Four
The *Dark Is Rising* Sequence (Wales)

The three settings of the *Dark Is Rising* sequence are Buckinghamshire, Susan Cooper's childhood home; Cornwall, the place where her family vacationed when she was a child; and North Wales, her grandparents' home and a place she often visited as a child.

For the Welsh setting, used in the last two books of the sequence, she chose the countryside surrounding the village of Aberdyfi, where her grandmother was born, her parents resided in their later years, and her aunt still lives. She says she took some liberties with the description of the area, "combining two valleys into one, but otherwise it's exact" (*DW,* 193). Wales is much the preferred setting in Cooper's thoughts; as an adult she has spent more time there than at the other two settings ("part of me is always there," she says [*DW,* 81]), and that is perhaps why the last two books become so heavily laden with Celtic lore, almost to the point, in the last book, of overflowing.

The Grey King

Cooper's fourth book of the *Dark Is Rising* sequence—more tightly structured than any of the other books—netted her the Newbery Award in 1976. The scenes are as dramatic and evocative as those in *Greenwitch,* but they are subtly integrated one with the other since there is not the strong tension of Wild Magic and human forces that exists with the Greenwitch and the painter. Here also the child character moves more clearly to the center of the conflict. Everything now falls to Will to succeed or fail in this quest; therefore, the unity of character, plot, and conflict is much stronger—and the child reader is pulled through the story more easily and quickly. *The Grey King* is also only slightly longer than *Greenwitch,* both books profiting from a simpler, more dramatic, story.

Part One: "The Golden Harp"

When Will Stanton goes to his Uncle David's farm in Wales to complete his recovery from a long illness (hepatitis); it is October, a significant time, as we will see, for the particular quest he will undertake. As his cousin Rhys drives him from the railway station to the farm, he feels he is in a part of Britain unlike any other he has known: "a secret, enclosed place, with powers hidden in its shrouded centuries."[1] On the way, they encounter a rough spot in the road (a large stone), which causes a flat tire. A passing motorist appears, a rough angry man named Caradog Prichard, who is particularly curious about Will's identity.

As they drive along, Rhys describes the low, hanging, ragged clouds Will sees as the "breath" of the Grey King, who, according to the old Welsh stories (known by both Cooper and her characters here) lives on the highlands nearby. Both happenings—the encounter with Caradog and Rhys's story of the Grey King—are important. The story jogs Will's memory about the chant he has forgotten during his illness and needs to remember. Observing Caradog causes him to wonder if the large stone that nearly wrecked the car has something to do with this strange, angry man.

The next day, roaming around the little gray town of Tywyn as Uncle David's car is being checked, Will's memory is jogged a little more. As he walks around town, he sees the Church of St. Cadfan, which causes words from the chant (something about Cadfan's Way) to surface in his mind. He decides he must find this "way" or road in order to piece together the riddle of the chant.

Uncle David advises him to ask another sheep farmer, John Rowlands, about Cadfan's Way, since he knows all about the old things of this place. Rowlands tells Will about an old road pilgrims once used (high places were safer to travel on, he says). Will begins a long walk around the edges of the farm and encounters a white dog with strange silver eyes that runs at him, causing him to fall. As the dog gazes into his eyes, "in a whirling instant" (*GK*, 22) he suddenly remembers everything from the verse that is his only guide for his quest. He also has an overwhelming feeling that there is danger for him in this Welsh Valley so close to the Old Way and the old "ways."

Then the next piece in the puzzle appears: the dog's owner is a boy with pale skin, white hair, and eyes the tawny color of a bird's eyes. The boy and the dog are both albino, set off as different, special, with magical traits at the outset. Until the boy explains, Will knows, but does not know how he knows, that the boy is named in the verse (the "raven

The Dark Is Rising Sequence (Wales)   51

boy"). His name is Bran, the Welsh word for *crow*, a bird linked to ravens. (Cooper borrows the name from Celtic myth; Bran was a ruler of Britain and son of Lir.) Surprisingly, the boy knows how Will knows to name him correctly: " 'It is because you are not properly human, but one of the Old Ones of the Light put here to hold back the terrible power of the Dark. You are the last of that circle to be born on earth. And I have been waiting for you' " (*GK*, 24).

Bran's words jog Will's memory, and he chimes in with more of the puzzle: " 'You see, it's the first quest, without help, for me' " (*GK*, 25). The Dark is rising, he continues, and they can win only with the right weapons, those made for them centuries before that must be gathered together for use in the final battle (Signs of the Light, grail, golden harp, and crystal sword). The quest for the harp is his own, Will explains. The quest for the grail and the manuscripts had been that of the Drew children, and the search for the Signs had been Will's—with Merriman's help. Barney found the grail, Simon saved it, and Jane retrieved the lead case. Now the quest will be Will's—with Bran's help—just as in the next and final book it will be Bran's quest—with Will's help. Thus children as the primary quest figures become the crucial factor for defining the sequence—or marketing it—as *children's* literature.

That the three verses from centuries before were never written down makes it all the more important to find a way back to them now, Will explains to Bran, and all the worse, illness has clouded his mind. That his illness may have been part of the Dark's plan begins to seem a strong possibility when he sees the dog's silver eyes have broken a spell (*GK*, 26), enabling him to remember.

Bran knows the first part of the chant himself; Merriman has been there before Will to tell him about the Dark and the Light, about Will, and about Bran's task—to help Will with his quest. Will then explains who Merriman is—his master, "the first of the Old Ones and the strongest, and the wisest" (*GK*, 28). (Will is Merriman's apprentice now, just as King Arthur once was.) Merriman will not take part in this quest, Will adds. There are too many missions for too many Old Ones just now, and Will is now able to assume responsibility for a quest; he is ready. Thus this book marks a break with the others of the sequence. Will comes into his own as a human boy and as an Old One of the Light, with the trust Merriman has bestowed on him. Will, for the first time, shoulders the problems himself.

Will and Bran begin to sort out more of the chant together. Each is important in crucial ways to the other: Bran is the native Welshman who knows the terrain; Will is the one with intuitive knowledge of the High Magic. Still Will has more to learn as he goes along in this quest, and how he takes on and succeeds in his learning as he engages in this new—and independent—quest is the focus of the book.

It is the week of Hallowe'en, the Celtic time of Samtane, celebrated on 31 October or 1 November as the festival marking both the beginning of winter and the Celtic New Year and the death of summer, when "time and space were temporarily frozen and normal laws suspended" and spirits of the "Otherworld" walked the earth" (Green, 55). (It also heralded the impending death of some of the Celts' herd animals, which were brought from the hills for slaughtering or breeding at this season.) In choosing this time of year for the book, Cooper thus sets the scene for the Grey King and the *milgwn,* the large gray foxes of the spirit world, to appear.

Bran knows that Hallowe'en in Welsh means the first day of winter, and he helps Will interpret one line of the chant: *"On the day of the dead, when the year too dies"* (*GK,* 26). He also teaches Will (and the reader) the meaning and pronunciation of Welsh words, thus producing a strong authenticity, and a stronger realism, for this legendary Celtic world that Will is entering.

At this point Caradog Prichard appears to accuse Bran's dog of chasing his sheep, and he threatens to shoot the dog if he catches it on his land. Bran replies that Caradog will incur bad luck if he does, and he advises him to look more closely at what is the work of foxes. When Caradog leaves, Bran tells Will more about this strange man and more about the Grey King and where he lives—on Cader Idris, a high mountain peak above this valley.

As Will roams the Welsh countryside on Hallowe'en, he begins to feel the anger of the Dark breaking through around him. This darkness becomes more visible when he witnesses one of John Rowlands's sheep as it is attacked, its throat ripped by something that looks like a silver dog. Rowlands leaves the sheep in a small, deserted cottage until he can herd the other sheep back; then he returns to find the cottage empty and no trail outside it, increasing Will's uneasiness. Bran suggests that this is the doing of the milgwn, large, fast, gray foxes from high up in the mountains of the Grey King, as he knows from the old stories. Will suddenly "sees" these enormous creatures of the Dark, like images on a screen—a warning, he decides, from the Old Ones to him.

Suddenly a fire breaks out on the mountain, and Will decides that the Grey King, the Brenin Llwyd (*llwyd* means gray) of legend, is walling off the mountain in order to keep them from finding the golden harp and waking the Sleepers, both named in the chant. Will and Bran see a white fox in the flames, but Bran mistakes the fox for his white dog, Cafall, and runs up the mountain after it. Will follows Bran to save him from his mistake, and soon they are both trapped behind a wall of flames as the fire swings northward. There they are surrounded by the milgwn and their leader, the king fox, with no escape except to climb to the mountain top.

Suddenly Cafall, Bran's dog, appears and begins to fight the foxes so that Will and Bran can escape; as they do so, they discover an overhanging cleft in the rocks (called Bird Rock) that Will manages, with a spell of the Old Speech, to open, as the verse-chant (or *gnome*) says he must do:

On the day of the dead, when the year too dies,
Must the youngest open the oldest hills
Through the door of the birds, where the breeze breaks . . . (GK, 58)

Suddenly they find themselves in a time-slip deep in the mountain, where they stand in the midst of blazing stars, observed by the High Magic of the Universe and examined for their right to claim the golden harp in this quest. Will feels too small to exist in the face of the night sky that wheels around them. *"Wish on a star"* (*GK,* 58), something within him enjoins. But when he begins to wish, nothing emerges in words. The star-filled sky then vanishes, and Will and Bran find themselves in a deep cavern of the mountain, where, by answering from rote memory questions posed by three of the Old Ones—a blue-eyed Lord (Arthur), Merriman, and a Lord of the Dark—they are given the golden harp. Will's wish thus comes true, but not because he is born to the High Magic (he continues to be observed and examined as he goes along, growing into his destiny). Rather, he is making his unspoken wish come true himself, through his own willpower, self-discipline, feelings of deep responsibility, intelligence, and hard work.

Then, at the moment when Arthur is speaking to Bran about his dog, Cafall, reassuring Bran of its safety from everyone except men of the earth, who alone can take life from one another, has his own work to do with the milgwn. Bran's playing of the harp wards off a storm of rage from the Grey King as they leave the cavern and try to go down the slope, wind, stones, branches flying at them with the strength of a tornado. Then a fox, seen only by Bran and Will, leaps at a sheep and tears its throat apart.

Caradog Prichard makes good his promise to shoot Cafall as the noble dog tries to fight the invisible fox. (Cooper has borrowed the name of Arthur's favorite dog, Cavall, as it appears in *The Mabinogion,* to bring the dog forward—as Cafall—in a time-slip.) The curtain rings down on this first half of the drama, with Bran suffering not just the loss of his dog but with Caradog's labeling of it as a sheep-killing dog, and Bran's father, Owen Davies, agreeing with him.

Only John Rowlands seems to have a grip on reality at this point. Even though the white fox has not been visible to his eyes, he notices that there is no blood on Cafall's mouth. Something did gore the sheep's throat, he says. But how could that be?

Part Two: "The Sleepers"

John Rowlands tells Will the story of Gwen, Bran's mother, who came out of the mountain in a freezing rainstorm, carrying Bran when he was only a few months old. In the three days she was there in this valley, she told no one about her past or her other home. She stayed at a cottage where Owen Davies lived and then disappeared, leaving Bran with Davies, who had fallen in love with her. She has never been seen since, " 'nor will she ever be' " (*GK,* 99), Rowlands says. Will learns that Caradog Prichard had also tried to involve himself with Gwen against her will, but Davies reached her in time to fight him off. Thus Caradog's shooting of the dog is part of this complicated set of events.

Will retrieves the harp that he hid in a shed near Caradog's farm. Wrapping the harp in an old sack, he sets off, only to meet the milgwn king. He immobilizes the great fox with an enchantment, just as a low mist begins to engulf him, and the gray-white fox changes to the color of Rowlands's dog Pen. The enchantment breaks, sending the now dark fox running off to Caradog's farm.

Again Will sets off with the harp only to find that now the harp is under enchantment, the weight of it dragging him to the ground. Then right before him, a mist whirls up into the huge shape of the Grey King, the most powerful Lord of the Dark. The Grey King speaks to Will, informing him that he may not complete his quest to wake the Sleepers, those warriors of Old Time who will be needed to rout the forces of the Dark at the last "rising" in the last book of the sequence. If he seeks the Sleepers, the Grey King says, he will be destroyed—and the harp, too. (Cooper's words—"wake the sleepers" [*GK,* 150]—are those of Prospero in Shakespeare's *The Tempest* Act 5, Scene 1: "Graves at my command have waked their sleepers.")

Will learns two things next: first, that the sack covering the harp—not the harp itself—is under enchantment by a white pebble called a "warestone," a magical object both the Dark and the Light use to spy on one another; second, that Caradog is not one of the Dark; he is simply being used by them. " 'A man so wrapped in his own ill-will is a gift to the Dark from the earth,' " says the king. " 'It is so easy to give him suitable ideas' " (*GK,* 108). Will, thinking no doubt of John Rowlands and Owen Davies, reminds him that " '[t]here are such men, of an opposite kind, who unwittingly serve the Light too' " (*GK,* 108). The king counters that the bad men outweigh the good.

The Grey King gives Will one night and one day to be gone from his land, and Will departs with the harp for Uncle David's farm. Because Caradog Prichard is threatening to kill his dog, Rowlands leaves early the next day with Will for another farm up in the valley where he assumes Pen will be safe. The farm is near a lake below Cader Idris, the mountain where the Grey King dwells. The lake is called Tal y Llyn, or "Pleasant Lake," and this same name appears in the verse-chant, where it signals the place where the Sleepers are.

Before Will leaves, Aunt Jen tells him more about Bran's mother, that she had had a serious misfortune in her past, having "betrayed a great trust"; thus she felt that "a second betrayal would be the end of the world" (*GK,* 114). As they drive along to the farm, Rowlands warns Will to be careful of what he does as a member of the Light because the Light sacrifices the one for the many. Rowlands says he would choose one human life above the many. Will admits he would, too, if he could, but he is fighting for humans, which means that the Dark must be stopped—at all costs. (The cost so far has been Cafall, a great misfortune for Bran.)

On a walk with Pen by Tal y Llyn, Will falls, injuring his arm (the Grey King's malevolence at work). Bran arrives on his bike to warn that Caradog is on his way to kill Pen. Bran and Will find refuge in the cottage where Will hid the harp (the same cottage where Owen Davies once lived for three days with Bran's mother and where he fought Caradog for menacing her). The Grey King fills the cottage with a strange malice, and Pen becomes the one enchanted, paralyzed by what Will suspects is a warestone hidden on the floor that has escaped his notice. He draws a circle around Pen and himself with a piece of wood; then he intones the words of a spell that turns the cottage dark and the ring around Pen and himself into cold firelight. A smaller blue light begins to glow and then blaze in a far corner of the room, and Will is certain that a warestone is present.

As he explains to Bran, a warestone is a small "thing" of power, used by both the Light and the Dark to observe each other and transmit the power of either. If it belongs to an Old One of the Light, it can transmit helpful power to Will; if it belongs to the Grey King, as Will decides that it does, then it would be able to paralyze Pen. Will is suddenly trapped: The Grey King will know everything they say or do while inside the cottage, a factor that adds to the suspense. Will he be able to escape this dilemma?

Bran volunteers to stay with Pen, a brave act since Caradog could come any moment and shoot the dog; Will cycles off to get the harp, the only hope he has for releasing the dog from its enchantment—another bold act, considering his injured arm. He wishes Merriman were there; the Old Ones can carry people, animals, and objects through place and time, something he has not yet learned how to do. With a lame arm, how will he manage the harp and the bike in the face of Caradog and the Grey King, he wonders.

In the cottage, Bran stares at the warestone. Then he goes to the door and stares off at Bird Rock, remembering the cavern where he met the blue-robed Lords. He thinks of the one who said the High Magic would never take Cafall from him: only humans through stupidity or greed would do so. He remembers the warmth of that one's understanding and "the eyes from the hooded face holding his own" (*GK,* 137). Filling his mind is resentment toward Will for causing Cafall's death, toward his father's strict, overprotective parenting, and against himself for being different. Cooper's creating Bran as an albino, facing the prejudices of others for his skin coloring, is a master stroke for introducing color as an issue. And since color is not connected to race in this story, she reveals more clearly how race is a social construct.

Fortunately, Bran's father arrives as this fury is building, and they begin to sort out past and present conflicts and puzzles together. Owen Davies tells Bran more than he ever has told him about Gwen and his own desperate search for her when she suddenly disappeared after three days in his cottage. Then for a moment, Bran turns against the mother who left him as he wonders "wildly: *Who am I?*" (*GK,* 145). Staring in the direction of the warestone, he sees the same blue light that Will invoked, shining out of the same corner of the room as when Will was there, and the room grows dark as before.

The blue light is an important connecting link in the magic Cooper is weaving between past and present time, since the light (the Light) is now imparting knowledge to Bran about his centuries-old past. In fact, it begins helping him enter a time-slip that Cooper indicates by doors opening, the same metaphor that we saw in *The Dark Is Rising* and also here in the mountain cavern of Bird Rock: "Bran had a strange jolting awareness of a part of his mind he had never been conscious of before. It was as if a door were opening somewhere within him, and he did not know what he would find on the other side. Flashing through his consciousness came a quick array of images, making no sense, like a dream dreamed while waking" (*GK*, 145). He sees scenes of his mother turning to leave him behind, her arms outstretched to him, and, finally, "the water of a distant lake glimmering like a lost jewel" (*GK*, 146).

Here is more of what John Rowlands refers to as the sacrifice of the one for the many: Gwen has given up mothering her child, and her child has given up his mother for the larger good that is needed for the Light's ongoing battle with the Dark. Bran must then emerge centuries later as the one to reclaim his father's sword, the only "thing" of power great enough to keep the Dark from rising the second—and last—time, as Merriman then knew. Therefore, he guided Gwen (Guinevere of Arthurian legend) in her decision to bring the boy forward in time, where he would remain safe from the ravages of greed, envy, mistrust, or betrayal in Arthur's time. As Aunt Jen, who knew the Gwen of this time and the long-ago legend of Arthur and Guinevere, has speculated, Gwen (the "reincarnated" Guinevere) was frightened of what might happen to the world itself if Arthur, or those around him, did not believe that Bran was really his son—or perhaps worse for him—if they *did* believe he was. (In either case war might result—from Guinevere's supposed adultery or the perceived power an heir would have over others.)

Bran can sense only glimpses of the pattern at this time, but in the new knowledge he has gained from these scenes of the past, he can begin to assert his power. Suddenly he wants to rejoin Will's quest and find his way to the lake below Cader Idris where the Sleepers must be awakened by the golden harp. There he might learn more about his past. He calls to Pen, and something in his voice, some new strength, releases the enchantment of the warestone; he and Pen run off to Tal y Llyn.

When Will arrives with the harp to find Bran and Pen gone, he cannot see who has broken the spell of the warestone. Surely not the Dark, who would not wish to do so. Surely not the Light, who have no power to do so. Surely not the Grey King, but whose power would be greater than his? Only the warestone can tell him, and it does, now that its power has been disconnected from its source, and no law of the Old Magic prevents it from doing so.

The warestone takes Will into a time-slip "in a series of images so rapid that they were like a narrative, a piece of a story" (*GK,* 149). First, he sees the clear blue eyes of the lord who questioned them at Bird Rock and for the first time met his son. Then he sees a grief-stricken woman feeling guilt; finally, connected to them both is Merriman. Then he sees an abbey and a man leading the woman carrying a baby from the abbey, followed by scenes of a high place, a cottage, and Owen Davies, younger than he is now, calling to the woman Gwen, who stands on the mountain, her arms empty now just as she is reentering the abbey. Finally he sees the blue-eyed man wearing a crown.

Will knows at last who Bran is and what Bran's destiny is, as well as his own: it is to be at Bran's side later when he comes fully into his power, as Merriman had been at Bran's father's side in King Arthur's own time. Will knows also how the Grey King's power over the warestone might have been broken—and by whom, if Bran saw what he is now seeing and realized at last who he was. If so, Will knows where Bran has gone.

At Tal y Llyn, below Cader Idris, Will encounters Caradog Prichard, who blocks his way, obsessed with finding Rowlands's dog. The Grey King is using Caradog's mind to force Will's hand. Will stands face-to-face with the power of the Grey King, who is protected by Caradog's human mind—even if Caradog's mind shatters, which it appears to be doing. Will tries an enchantment (an image of a wild sea filled with leaping fish surging at Caradog) to drive the man back, but to no avail. His only hope is to play the harp. Sweeping his hand over the strings, "the world changed" (*GK,* 157). The centuries-old horsemen, silver-gray, ghostly, awaken to ride down out of Cader Idris to restore the world. Each of the Sleepers salutes Bran with his sword, as son of Arthur before they rise into the sky.

At the same time, the harp causes Caradog Prichard to recall Gwen playing a golden Welsh harp, so he heaves the harp into the lake in retaliation for her rejection of him years before. In his wrath he cries out that he, instead of Owen Davies, could have taken the child, and Bran responds with the most poignant line of the book: " 'And would you then have shot my dog Cafall, Mr. Prichard?' " (*GK,* 163). Bran then recalls that his father had a dog named Cafall, and Will knows that he knows now who he is—Arthur's heir and Owen Davies's son.

Davies then tells of naming his dog for Arthur's own dog, of knowing who Gwen was and that she came from Cader Idris, the "Seat of Arthur" (*GK,* 164) through an enchantment. Bran and his human

The Dark Is Rising *Sequence (Wales)*

father embrace as the final curtain rings down on this scene of reconciliation, all fury spent by Caradog's last shriek of madness, the Dark having faded away with the last glimpse of the risen Sleepers, and the ghostly gray foxes disappearing into the darkened lake.

Silver on the Tree

The last book of the *Dark Is Rising* sequence is the richest and perhaps the most satisfying of all these books, at least for the adult reader. Cooper had at this point settled in with her characters, and they had settled in with one another. But she was balancing a great many things: all the ideas about her worldview and the particular aspects of the entire quest pattern of the books. In addition, she had created a huge cast of characters: Will's family, consisting of nine children and his parents, the three Drew children, various adults—family, neighbors, townspeople of the different settings—and the legendary characters of both England and Wales that are interwoven throughout the entire set of books. It was a huge undertaking, and we will see, as we sort through it here, how it all plays out.

Part One: "When the Dark Comes Rising"

The book opens on a hot midsummer day in England with one of the most arresting scenes of the sequence, one designed to show the time-slip aspect of the fantasy. It also unveils Will's place in the quest as an Old One with special powers to see and understand that which ordinary humans cannot know. Lying idly in the grass, he sees swans on the river where he and his brothers, Stephen and James, have gone fishing, "slow-moving white shapes, drifting back upstream" (*ST,* 3). One of the swans passes behind Stephen, who is "standing tall a few yards off . . . But as it passed, it did not disappear behind Stephen. Will could see the white form clearly through the outline of Stephen's body" (*ST,* 3).

Stephen and the swan each become mere outlines, and through them both, Will sees "a steep slope of land, grassy, without trees, that had not been there before" (*ST,* 3) and a group of small, dark-haired figures (Celtic people of a distant time running to escape a foreign invasion). A little later in his sighting, he sees these people bury bundles filled with gold cups and plates, jewels, candlesticks, and silk woven with gold into a deep hole at the top of a hill. They cover the hole with a flint boulder and flee.

Back once again in his own time, lying in the grass, Will sees a small, dark animal that he thinks is a weasel or stoat, and it causes him to feel "a pulsing ferocity of viciousness and evil so strong that his mind rebelled against believing it could exist" (*ST,* 9). Stephen is suddenly reminded of something he needs to sort out with Will. While in the Navy, Stephen has been stationed in Jamaica. There in the middle of Carnival, a Jamaican man, a stranger, has sent a message to Will (through Stephen) that the Old Ones of the ocean islands are ready. Further, another stranger Stephen met in Gibraltar has sent a similar message from the South. (Those different places—and faces—signify worldwide brotherhood of the Light.)

Will proceeds to explain everything to Stephen about the Light, the Dark, the Old Ones, the Old Magic, the Wild Magic, and the High Magic. But Stephen becomes even more confused. Does Will really believe these fantasies? Is he—Stephen—dreaming or going crazy? Will explains that the messages had to come as they did—unwritten and in secret—to keep them safe from the Dark. Then he realizes that it is up to him to keep the secrets of the High Magic safe one time more (foreshadowing the ending of this book and the sequence when the mortal children will be "caused" by Great-Uncle Merry to forget all they have seen in their quest-adventures for the Light). So he invokes a flood of white plume moths to carry away his brother's memories of their talk.

James soon appears to talk about the mink, which he says was originally brought over from America to be bred for fur, but a few escaped and "went wild" (*ST,* 15). On returning home, they encounter a Sikh child being bullied by some classmates, English boys whose parents' prejudice toward immigrants has undermined their own humanity. They grab the boy's violin, and Will tells them to give it back. In response, one boy heaves it into a stream (echoes of Caradog Prichard throwing the magical harp into the lake in Wales). Stephen reacts by heaving the boy himself into the stream and ordering him to retrieve the case, which he does. Thus, if music is the "door" into the spirit world, they have kept the door from slamming shut when they saved both Manny Singh and his violin—at least for the moment.

Back at home, they discover that minks have invaded their own chicken house, killing "for the love of it" (*ST,* 23), Will says, when James recalls that the mink is the only animal, except for the polecat, that does not kill just when it is hungry. As Stephen and James set to work to repair the hen-run, Will, hearing their hammers ringing rhythmically, feels the whirling take hold of his mind again, and the sound of the hammering changes to a hollow sound of iron striking iron. Will staggers against the barn wall as the moon disappears and enters "a time-slip so complete that in an instant he could see no trace of Stephen or James, nor any familiar thing or animal or tree" (*ST,* 24).

He finds himself in the presence of Merriman and Arthur, who are planning the battle of Badon after three hundred of the "best men of Britain" (*ST,* 25) have been slaughtered. They welcome him as the last and youngest of the Old Ones. This is the first rising, when Arthur must win a battle that stands as the first great rising of the Dark. The second occurs 15 centuries later when Will has been human-born and his part in the quest means engaging in past events in order to change them.

To save the modern world from total immersion in the Dark, Will, who has earlier achieved the joining of the six Signs of the Light into a circle, must now call the members of the Circle of the Light from around the world. As two of these Old Ones have already told Stephen, they are ready to help the humans of the world in both Arthur's time and this one, when the Dark is rising again. The calling of the Old Ones serves both "times" since, in the Circle of the Light, all time is one. Will sees that he must go outside of Time to retrieve the Signs he has previously hidden. If he does not, Merriman reminds him, the High Magic that guards them will take them outside Time (they will be forever inaccessible), and the Dark will have the advantage.

Will returns to his own world and time to consider how he will retrieve the Signs. The task requires creating for himself a time-slip, since that was the way he had hidden the Signs. He stares into the same painting that took him back into Roman times before; it is a dark Victorian print hanging in the front hall of his home in Buckinghamshire, entitled "The Romans at Carleon," a panoramic scene showing the construction of an amphitheater, 16 centuries earlier.

When he time-traveled there soon after returning home at the end of *The Dark Is Rising,* he and Merriman entered the scene of the picture through a magical spell, and we see in a flashback what happened then. As a slab of rock was lowered into place, Will slipped off his belt, through which was threaded the six Signs, or cross-quartered circles (bronze, iron, wood, gold, flint, and crystal) and dropped it into a slot where the next stone slab of the amphitheater would fit and a "coffin" of stone would hold the Signs safely.

This scene did not appear in any of the earlier books of the sequence, and, because flashbacks are not a typical strategy for Cooper, it seems oddly placed here. The scene might have been written for *The Dark Is*

Rising but ultimately omitted; at least it belongs with the action of that book, although it would have been awkward to include it unless written as an epilogue. As it stands, the flashback tends to clutter the action and cloud the focus. A better solution, in terms of narrative shaping, would have resulted from condensing this chapter, "The Calling," and turning it into a prologue leading directly into part 2 of this book—with all the other chapters of this section deleted.

Part Two: "The Singing Mountains"

Jane Drew and Will Stanton meet on a hillside above the village of Aberdyfi, Wales. *Silver on the Tree* really needs to begin right here—with Jane hearing music and setting off to discover what it is. (Actually, Will is playing the small, curved hunting horn that he received at the end of *The Dark Is Rising*.) He has arrived at Aunt Jen's house once again, just as the Drew children have arrived for a vacation in Aberdyfi, the place where their great-grandfather had originally lived.

Soon the Drew children encounter Will's friend Bran, whose father, Owen Davies, rents a cottage on Uncle David's farmland, and Will explains their mission for this new quest—to find the Lady, the "greatest [Old One] of all" (*ST,* 69). The children discuss where they will look for her and settle on a walk into the hills above Aberdyfi (or Aberdovey— *aber* meaning *the mouth of, the estuary of*) between the Happy Valley and the Dyfi (or Dovey) River, where Jane suddenly becomes hesitant to continue the mission since none of them knows how things will proceed. Bran's reaction is anger: " 'If you have seen the raising of fear, and the killing of love, and the Dark creeping in over all things [as he has seen in *The Grey King*], you do not ask stupid questions' " (*ST,* 83) like what am I doing here? You keep going to *discover* what you will do.

Unconvinced by his reasoning and filled with fear and resentment about his tone, Jane wanders off alone, ending up back at the Bearded Lake, where she hears distant singing from across the valley. She recognizes Will's voice and then another voice, an echo, a "ghostly second voice" (*ST,* 89) mixed with his. It is as if the mountains are singing. At this moment, the figure of the Lady appears—but only for human eyes, as Merriman had predicted. In this particular time-slip, the present-day human child does not just go back into the past or even see scenes from the past, as Will and Bran can; the past comes to her: "The brightness grew more intense until suddenly it was all contained in a glowing rose-coloured stone set into a ring, and the ring on the finger of a slender figure standing before her . . . Jane had forgotten the others, forgotten the mountain and the rain" (*ST,* 90).

It was intended from the beginning, the Lady says, that Jane should carry this last message: " 'Some things there are that may be communicated only between like and like . . . For you and I are much the same, Jane, Jana, Juno, Jane, in clear ways that separate us from all other concerned in this quest' " (*ST,* 90–91). According to Goodrich, "The Irish syllable *an* . . . in a lady's name is also identical . . . with the Latin name of the Roman god Janus . . . [who] goes back to the days of the ancient, migratory Celts of Italy" (224). In other words "like to like" means not just female to female, but female as patron and protector of women, as Juno and the historical Guinevere (as opposed to the Guinevere of medieval romance) both would have been.

Thus Cooper appears to be blending the two Guineveres in the sequence. In *The Grey King,* she relied on medieval Arthurian romances, written, for example, by Thomas Malory and Chrétien de Troyes, in which the sexual triangle of Arthur, Lancelot, and Guinevere becomes a dominant focus. For those books in which the Lady appears (*The Dark Is Rising* and *Silver on the Tree*), Cooper enlarges the portrait of Guinevere or enables it to blend with the figure of the Mother Goddess.

Jane is to tell Will that he and Bran must go to the Lost Land at the moment "when it shall show itself between land and the sea." A "white bone" will "prevent" them, and a "flying may-tree" will save them; "only the horn can stop the wheel." And in the "glass tower," among seven trees, they will find "the crystal sword of the Light" (*ST,* 91). Then she tells Jane one thing more before fading from sight: to "be brave" (*ST,* 91).

This advice is particularly apt, for suddenly a great, slimy, horned serpent rises out of the Bearded Lake, swaying close to Jane as if to strike her. This agent of the Dark causes Jane's mind to feel the evil ("its will groping for hers" [*ST,* 94]). It commands her to tell it the Lady's message. She resists and then faints from the exertion of resisting. Bran, sensing trouble, rushes to Jane and faces down this creature that calls itself the *afanc* of Llyn Barfog. The other children realize that the afanc is like a nightmare, powerless except to make threats. (Evil is in the mind, and if we bring mind over matter, we can face it down.)

Bran's command to the afanc causes Jane to sense that he is more than he seems. When she asks Will about him, he tells her Bran's story: Bran is Arthur's son by Guinevere, who "brought him forward in Time" (*ST,* 97) to be reared by an adopted father in modern times because she feared Arthur would not accept him as the true heir (her past with Lancelot, according to the legend, might have made him feel he was once again being deceived).

Feeling pride in having been chosen by the Lady as message bearer for the quest, Jane tells Will what they must do, and they begin searching for the Lost Land. As they climb the slope above the lake, they quickly see it, since the Lady has appeared where they are to be—*Cors Fochno,* the flat land on the other side of the river. They realize where they are when Bran tells a centuries-old story of the Lowland Hundred, the fertile but flat land of King Gwyddno Garanhir, who was "drowned" (or *lost*) when the seawall broke.

Will senses the High Magic all around them, a "kind of intoxication, a wonderful expectancy of marvelous things" (*ST,* 102). Suddenly, as they all stand watching, Jane sees the sea fall back, and the Lost Land reveals itself, with "trees, and flowers, and walls and buildings of grey stone, blue slate and glimmering gold" (*ST,* 103) rising up before them. She notices the air suddenly drawing itself into a ribbon-road, onto which Will and Bran can step and move over the river onto land.

The Drew children cannot follow, since they are not out of legend like Bran or one of the Old Ones like Will. Cooper takes them instead into a time-slip of history, but, filled as it is with so many additional characters and incidents, it tends to muddy the narrative waters when the stream of story should be rushing on to the Lost Land.

Part Three: "The Lost Land"

Into the deepest time-slip possible—that of a long-ago legendary time and a lost-forever place, go Bran and Will in search of the crystal sword of the Light. This is a world—in many ways an inner, subconscious world—of wishes and dreams, especially those of the king of this lost "Atlantis," Gwyddno Garanhir.

According to Spivack, there is an ancient Welsh poem in which a mythical prince, Gwyddneu, rules over a lost country, now submerged in the waters of Cardigan Bay (48). Cooper, however, doubles the significance of *lost* by having Gwyddno Garanhir suggest the Fisher King of medieval Arthurian romance, utilizing the Grail theme or quest-journey to self-knowledge. (With this theme, an old king who has lost all confidence in his power to rule has withdrawn into a Grail Castle, a place filled with terror and enchantment, in a land that lies fallow, reflecting the loss of the king's own power and fertility. A questing hero must save the king and the land by passing certain tests, one of which is that he be chaste and pure hearted.)

The pilgrimage the two boys make to Gwyddno's inner world unravels in seven scenes or settings: City, Library-Theater, Rose-Garden, Palace, Stone House, Castle of Glass (Caer Wydyr), and Glass Tower. First, the shining ribbon-road leads them down onto a golden roof overlooking a great city. Climbing down gray stone stairs, they are met by two saddled horses and taken through stone-paved streets to a wooden door that swings open into a narrow corridor. Their situation feels neither bad nor good, and Will remembers that neither the Dark nor the Light has any power in this land.

Next they climb a ladder to a long gallery composed of various levels. It is half library, where people stand browsing through books with blank pages, and half theater. A mocking audience causes Will to feel overwhelmed until Bran shouts out their mission that they have come for Eirias (words he remembers that mean *fire* or *blaze*). The audience falls silent and disappears. Will and Bran are then escorted by a small, bearded man named Gwion, who knows all about them and their mission but cannot give them answers or tell them what to do. He can only counsel them to trust their intuition and remember certain things that will help them in the quest.

A blue coach drives them to a rose garden, on the door of which is the king's crest: a leaping fish, "a Dyfi salmon" (*ST,* 154) between three roses. According to Fife, the Celts considered water an enchanted place since humans could not breathe there, and they found fish fascinating since they could breathe under water. The salmon was particularly attractive to Celtic warriors since it was "a strong creature, handsome, audacious and cunning" and "peerless" (Fife, 124) in its ability to leap upstream. Also, it was thought to fill the warrior with wisdom since it ate nuts from the hazel tree (the tree of wisdom), thus its name, the Salmon of Knowledge.

On the way Bran and Will are pursued by Riders of the Dark, or those absorbed in or obsessed by extremist views. They are "blinded by their own shining ideas," Will says, "or locked up in the darkness of their own heads" (*ST,* 146); thus they are dressed in cloaks of both black and white. The Riders tell Bran they will prevent his taking of Eirias, and Will recalls a previous victory for the Light, when the Wild Hunt faced down the Dark in England (in *The Dark Is Rising*).

The colors of the Riders and their talk of victory, alongside Will's vision of them as "images from a chessboard" (*ST,* 146), may put us in mind once again of a game of light and dark that Cooper is creating for readers to "play" alongside the characters she has placed on this "board." Readers then feel like those of Celtic times, when board games (unearthed in Britain and Ireland), called *brandubh* or *tawbwrdd,* showed man's place in the world in opposition to a "hostile Otherworld" (Ellis 1994, 236).

In this garden Gwion suddenly appears beside a fountain to reassure them that the Dark knows all but can do little in the Lost Land (fear and evil are a state of mind here). In the fountain water, they see a vision of a man holding a crystal sword. The man is the king, Gwion tells them, and his image is projected to them from the glass tower by those of the Light. They see writing engraved on the marble fountain, a line that Gwion advises them to remember: *"I am the womb of every holt"* (*ST,* 153).

The blue, driverless coach takes them to the king's empty palace, filled with a maze of mirrors that Bran finds sobering and distasteful, a blank wall of himself, stopping him from going forward. (According to Fife, glass was a rare material for the Celts, and therefore, magical. Early glass was "thick and watery" [47] because it was filled with impurities; it came to symbolize the separation of the living from the dead because of the murky reflections and light distortions.)

Will suggests that they should be remembering something, and when Will recalls the words written on the fountain, new words appear on the mirror (*"I am the blaze on every hill"* [*ST,* 160]), the glass walls shatter, and Will and Bran are released from the maze. (How does one break out of the living "death" of self-absorption? By talking to others, remembering their words and advice, and most of all by keeping commitments.)

Gwion reappears to commend them on finding their way, and Will notices that Gwion wears a ring on which is carved a leaping fish (the salmon of the king's crest). Gwion tells the story of how the sword Eirias was made for the Light and how the sword maker fell prey to his own uncertainties and feelings of inadequacy (human fear of all kinds is an important subject for Cooper). He also discloses how the maker has ever since been imprisoned by his own mind, an artist's mind, always ripe for self-doubts and prey to loss of confidence. When the artist is also the king, as in this case, "the mind can produce giant spectres of great power," (*ST,* 166) Gwion adds as he leads them back into the library-theater that turns out to be placed at the center of the empty palace.

The room has changed; in shattering the glass walls, Bran and Will broke a barrier—that of human *life.* Now the room is filled with warmth, conversation, art, literature—and words on the pages of the books. Opening one book, they see the Lady as a young woman, standing in front of the fountain of the rose garden; across from her picture on the facing page are words that Gwion advises them to remember: *"I am the queen of every hive"* (*ST,* 169).

Two golden horses wait to take them to the next place—the glass castle of the Lost Land. On the way, Bran compares Jane to a girl in the crowd who throws a red rose to Will, and we learn that it is Bran, not Will, who thinks of Jane—and thinks of her as pretty. (Their earlier altercation, in part 2, is seen now as signaling—or foreshadowing—mutual attraction.)

Will sees the Riders of the Dark at their backs; they are then overtaken by the skeleton of a horse ("the white bone that will prevent them" of the Lady's message). This is the *Mari Llwyd* of Celtic legend, except that the entire skeletal body of the horse is present instead of just the skull. (Heads and skulls of horses played a prominent role in Celtic myth, especially in tricking or frightening one's enemies, since severed heads were perceived to have "magical properties" [Green, 71].)

Fighting off paralyzing fear, Will and Bran take refuge in a little gray stone house outside which a blossoming hawthorn grows. As the horse wheels laughing before the house, they remember the Lady's words about a "flying may-tree." Then the hawthorn petals fall on the horse, collapsing it, as words appear on the wooden door, *"I am the shield of every head"* (*ST,* 178).

In the cottage Will finds a small mirror in which Merriman appears to urge Will on to the finish, his absence resulting from the need to save Simon when the children entered the time-slip at the wharf and Simon fell—or was pushed—into the water. Merriman tells Will to remember the Lady's words and other things he is told in the Lost Land, to trust Gwion, and to be assured that those of the Light will be with them when they bring back the crystal sword, the last "thing" of Power in these quests.

The Dark surrounds them as they set out for the last part of the journey, and a boat sails by to take them to Caer Wydyr, the king's glass castle. Gwion is also on the boat, and once on land he begins collecting twigs from the seven trees (mentioned in the Lady's message to Jane) for each of them to carry. Each tree has a special value for their needs, he explains: Alder is the tree of fire; willow, the enchanter's tree; birch, an old tree; oak, a sturdy one; hazel has healing powers; apple is for food; and holly has sharp spines. He also explains more about the Lost Land, a hard—and frightening—place of the Wild Magic, he says, that has given birth to the *Mari Llwyd*.

Bran is convinced he has been here before, and Gwion says Bran was born here. (Bran, as legendary British ruler of Arthurian times, is said to have had a palace on the coast of Cornwall or "submerged below the waves, an Atlantis, a Caer Siddi 'Castle of Glass' " [Fife, 124].) Since Bran is Guinevere and Arthur's son and the sword Eirias was made here for the Light, at Arthur's request, Bran later says, then the Lost Land seems to suggest a place like Camelot, "a medieval dream city that never existed anywhere" (Ashe, 81) but different from the gentle, romanticized "Camelot" of modern fairy tales and Broadway show tunes.

Wedded as it is here to the legend of Atlantis, the sense of loss surrounding a place and time that is vanished forever is strengthened. Bran and Will have stepped into this deepest and most complex time-slip of all—a lost place in past time—a place they have brought back to life by slipping back into it from their own modern world.

The Dark Rider appears again to taunt Bran. The door of Caer Wydyr is barred by a large wheel, a quartered circle, spinning with deadly speed. The test of remembering falls now to Will and Bran, just as it fell to Jane to remember the words of the Lady's message. Merriman is not there to help them, and Gwion cannot give them any clues. His eyes simply prod Will to think. But in this game of Dark and Light, Will knows the winning play. He asks Bran for the last words of the Lady's message, and Bran remembers, "*Only the horn can stop the wheel.*" Will reaches for his little hunting horn; he plays a single note, and the spinning stops. As they step through the wheel, Will seizes the twigs, throws them through the spokes, and the spinning starts up again, preventing the Dark from following them into the tower.

In the castle, they discover the old king in the glass tower, and they plead for him to give them the crystal sword, for the Dark is rising and they of the Light must be armed with "all the Things of Power" (*ST,* 200) made for their purpose. The Celtic vegetation gods could bring slain warriors back to life, or "wake the Sleepers" in Cooper's words, through the magical properties of their treasures: cup, lance, sword, and stone (Fife, 130). Cooper's "Things of Power" are a cup of knowledge, the Signs of cultural history of the land, a harp of spirituality, and a sword of power to save a lost land. But they serve the same purpose. They can also be related to the Jungian principle of individuation. Cowan lists the quest objects as sword, cauldron, cup, and fairy lover, and he describes them as "symbols of psychic wholeness, health, and the integrated soul" (Cowan, 161).

Here the king, wearing a ring with a leaping fish—like Gwion's—is petulant and filled with his own grief and self-absorption (the Fisher King). But Bran takes command, rising to the glory of his destiny and his birthright to lead others. When the King sees Bran, he remembers a dream he once had of a boy bringing his father's greatness to the world.

Bran brings together all the lines of the chant they have been collecting on their journey from the walls of fountain, palace, library, stone house, and now the castle tower. He recites the poem, and the words appear above the place where they finally see, behind a wooden screen, the crystal sword. At this point the king relinquishes Eirias to its destined owner. Pointing across the room to a chest on which is painted in blue the picture of a man riding a fish, the king asks Gwion to open it and draw out a scabbard for Bran and a "small bright harp" (*ST,* 205) that he made long ago for "my Gwion, my Taliesin, for my player" (*ST,* 206).

Naming the king Gwyddno, Cooper links the legends of the Fisher King to that of Taliesin, the legendary Welsh bard, for Gwyddno, in Celtic myth, is the father of a youth named Elffin, who, while fishing one day, finds a baby in a stream. The baby grows up to win favor with King Arthur as the bard Taliesin, who had been reborn in the myths from a past existence when he was called Gwion Bach. As the old story went, Gwion Bach was chased by his mother, who was herself a shaman shape changer. Because he had tasted the magic of her cauldron, he changed himself first into a fish, then into a bird, and finally into a grain of wheat that his mother, having changed herself into a hen, swallowed. Later she gave birth to the baby that Elffin (son of Gwyddno) finds. And, as we just mentioned, that baby grows up to become Taliesin, a famous sixth-century bard or poet-singer for the court and a "prophetic" poet at that (Ellis 1992, 205).

Are Will and Bran in the company of the famous bard himself? Is Gwion of the Lost Land a reincarnation of Gwion Bach? Very possibly, since ancient Celtic people believed in the transmigration or immortality of souls: The soul did not disappear or perish but simply passed from the old body to a newer one after death, "a kind of rebirth" (Green, 72) or migration of the soul through a number of different births. We need not assume that Cooper is attempting to put forth such a philosophical notion, however, to enjoy the way such story embeddings reflect the layers of identity that arise from such beliefs or from Cooper's skill in weaving rich tapestries of mythic fantasy. None of her stories is richer than this one of Gwion and Gwyddno and the day they pass quietly and proudly into Time.

As darkness begins to fill the sky of the Lost Land this day, the end of their time and place is nearing. Will and Bran have entered the past to share a moment of that time, and when the Lost Land is truly lost, when it sinks into the sea, they will be there to witness this singular occurrence. So they see how it all ended: with the people laughing and dancing in the face of their doom, Gwion playing the harp for his king, and the frail king leaning on the balcony wall, listening with joy to the gentle notes. As the sea rises and Bran and Will jump back into the little boat that brought them, lightning strikes the castle tower, but Gwion refuses to leave, telling them to go and save Eirias; he will stay since he belongs there.

After a violent storm in which they are tossed into unconsciousness, Bran and Will wake at last on the sand of the River Dyfi, where the sun is rising and Jane has slipped out to be on the beach at sunrise, as Merriman has told her to do.

Part Four: "Sunrise"

When all five children meet together on the beach, Simon asks Will what he wants them to do, and Will advises them to trust their own judgment. The Dark cannot destroy humans, he reminds them; it can only cause them to destroy themselves if they use poor judgment. At this point the sand whirls up, and out comes the White Rider, taking Barney off into a time-slip, in this case one of history, that of Owain Glyndwr's time—twelfth-century Wales, when his rebellion against the English took place.

Barney is accused of spying for the English King Henry, but Bran and Will arrive soon to rescue him. Hope is alive among these Welshmen, who may foresee their defeat. However, as Glyndwr tells Will, if the Circle extends as far forward as their twentieth century, with Norman, Saxon, and Dane having found a way to live together in peace, then their own failure in this earlier time is not so hopeless.

Soon the three boys find themselves back in their own time, where they meet Jane and Simon on a "time-train" (*ST,* 228) carrying all the Old Ones of the Light. They are traveling across the island of Britain to the Midsummer Tree, in the Chiltern Hills of England, where, Merriman explains, whoever cuts the "blossom, at the moment when it opens fully from the bud, shall turn events and have the right to command the Old Magic and the Wild Magic, to drive all rival powers out of the world and out of Time" (*ST,* 240).

People of all times, places, and cultures are on this train, as well as many of the characters that the children have encountered in their adventures. This is the "rising," Merriman explains to Jane. " 'And the danger will grow now' " (*ST,* 233), but she need not be afraid. The Dark will not harm them, since one of their own is on this train.

Jane's perspective carries the reader through this part of the book; it is her empathetic "gift" that takes readers more deeply into John Rowlands's feelings as he awakens to the treachery of his wife, Blodwen, one of the Dark. Merriman must evict her from this train of Time, and when he does, she lands on the white horse, revealing herself to be the White Rider who earlier abducted Barney. This is a problematic scene; Blodwen's villainy is not foreshadowed strongly enough. It remains especially unconvincing now, since nothing in either *Greenwitch* or *Silver on the Tree,* in which Blodwen appears, really explores her character in enough depth to prepare us for the double agent "career" choice she has made.

Her name might be significant; it seems to emerge from Blodeuwedd of pre-Christian Celtic lore. The Fourth Branch of the *Maginogi* recounts a story in which Math and a magician, Gwydion, make a wife for Lleu Llaw Gyffes from flowers; and when "Blodeuwedd, born without roots and thus without moral sense, is faithless, she and her lover Gronw Pebr conspire to murder Lleu" (Green, 34). Later, as her punishment, she is turned into an owl. The word *Blodeuwedd* means *owl,* says the teller in this story. So Blodeuwedd is condemned to hunting alone at night, just as Cooper's Blodwen is sent to live permanently among the Dark and is hated by the birds.

Blodwen Rowlands's faithlessness does not seem to have a sexual component. She simply seems to be an ambitious woman who wanted power of some kind and found it by being a White Rider. In other words, Cooper may simply be using the name to send echoes of a faithless female who loses everything for her self-aggrandizing tendencies (which Blodeuwedd may or may not have had). The convention of using legendary names to "round out" a minor character does work to some degree. It also serves to keep male and female villainy in balance. We have far more male scoundrels than female in the sequence; even the Greenwitch is a character that we see empathetically, the result, perhaps, of Jane's own empathetic response to her.

Perhaps we simply need more development of Jane's perspective on Blodwen. But there is no time for it; this "vehicle of the Light" (*ST,* 240) is rushing on eastward to the tree, carrying Eirias. Since it is a two-edged sword (it may be possessed by the Dark as well as the Light), two things are needed now: for Bran to keep the sword safe and for the six of them to keep Bran safe. In a boat now, they and John Rowlands lurch about on a river; actually, they have entered another time-slip, which Barney describes as "the best kind of dream" *ST,* 241). They are part of a contingent of vessels engaged in the Battle of Badon, what Merriman describes as the "first making and breaking of your land" (*ST,* 243).

A boat arrives bearing King Arthur, who addresses Bran as his son and then passes the linked Signs to Will, whom he calls "Sign-seeker" (*ST,* 244). Arthur invites Bran to come with him in his ship, *Pridwen* (the name comes from Arthur's ship in Celtic myth, called the *Pridwen,* meaning "fair face"[2]), to his castle, for their great victory this day against the Dark will not last long. He continues in this vein, telling what happens in the future: the Peace of Arthur lasts for a few years before the Saxons come and everything of the Old World vanishes.

Merriman then enters, reporting that men are fleeing to the west, one man carrying a grail that foretells, in an inscription, how a future world will fight the Dark that will rise not by bloodshed but through cold-blooded men. (Cooper leaves such crimes to the reader's imagination, but problems like environmental abuse, world hunger, and injustices resulting from racist, sexist, and classist beliefs, or prejudices, come to mind.)

Arthur sails on, and a Black Rider appears to challenge Bran's right to the sword, since Bran was taken out of his own time at his birth and placed in a future time to be reared, although it was not a time of his mother's choosing. Merriman loaded the dice in favor of the Light (encouraging Gwen to give up her son) in order to save Bran for this time of the Dark's second rising. Then Bran could move into his power as the Pendragon, when his power was needed most. As the Lady appears standing on the prow of the ship to negotiate the dispute, Bran is encased in a "cage of light" (*ST,* 249). John Rowlands is chosen by the Dark to judge the challenge; Merriman will defend the Light, and the Black Rider will speak for the Dark.

Merriman says Bran is attached to his own time and the people of that time. " 'Such loving bonds,' " he adds, " 'are outside the control even of the High Magic, for they are the strongest thing on all this earth' " (254). John Rowlands rules in favor of Bran since Bran is a valued member of his own modern time and has chosen freely to work for the Light. Bran should remain a member of their cause, says Rowlands, with freedom to help them further if he so chooses.

The boat and the members of the Circle of Light move on; suddenly they find themselves in green fields (the Chiltern Hills). The mist has blown away, and an oak tree covered silver with mistletoe appears in the distance (thus the title of this book). When each flower is in bloom, Bran, protected by the others (each of whom holds one of the Signs), must cut the spray. But before Will can remove the necklace of Signs, the Dark comes looming over them. Only the power of the Sleepers, led by Herne the Hunter, with his Wild Hunt and Hounds of Doom, is strong enough to defend them. Simon shouts that the tree is bursting into bloom. Then as the Riders loom closer to Earth, Will tears off the necklace, and Merriman and the children move into action, each taking a different Sign. The last flower bursting open, Bran cuts the mistletoe, and the Riders—and the Signs—both disappear.

As Green notes, "On the sixth day of the moon the druids climbed a sacred oak and cut off a mistletoe bough using a 'golden' (probably bronze gilded) sickle, catching the branch in a white cloak" (65). Mistletoe was used as a remedy for infertility, and the cutting, coming as it does here, so soon after Will and Bran's journey through the Lost Land, implies curing the world of evil, which had rendered the land barren. Says Fife, "Mistletoe is a phallic emblem [having] to do with fertility and the rites of manhood and male initiation into the elite warrior caste . . . Fertility depended on action, insertion, thrust; hence the symbolism of sword and lance in *all* primitive religions" (157).

Herne the Hunter leaps across the sky at the very moment that Arthur's ship appears. Will sees in Herne's head the tawny eyes of an owl. Later he will think of Bran's similar tawny owl's eyes and wonder if, in a different time, Bran and Herne were the same person. Yet there is "a look of Arthur too," he notices, "as if all three were one and the same" (*ST,* 269). Cooper is reinventing the Arthurian myth, in other words, not only to include Bran in the story but also to endow Bran with the fierce caring of both Herne and Arthur he will need to lead others in the modern world.

Arthur kneels before the Lady who may be, in different times, the same person as Gwen (Guinevere), Arthur's queen in each of the different legendary "hives"—Celtic, French, Scottish—that claim her as their own cultural heroine. She comes forward to his boat with a "beckoning touch on Arthur's arm in the casual closeness of those who belong to the same family" (*ST,* 265) to say " 'It is done' " (*ST,* 265). Guinevere would have been both a member of Arthur's family and would have had a commitment to see that "it" was done, whether "it" signifies the completion of Arthur's work or the completion of it by their son, Bran, whom she moved into another time so that he could do what he has done this day: use the crystal sword to cut the silver mistletoe from the tree.

The Lady smiles at the children, especially at Jane, remembering Jane's vital role in carrying the message that has set this last quest in motion (and also perhaps seeing Jane as Bran's future bride). Then she bestows on John Rowlands the gift of forgetting his wife's betrayal. Arthur invites Bran to join them in entering this great ship Pridwen, filled with "ghostly throng of beings . . . [that] he had known, on this journey and on other journeys, in this time and other times" (*ST,* 267), including the King of the Lost Land and his bard Gwion, now that the great mission is complete.

But Bran chooses, like Gwion, to stay where he feels he belongs, where he has "loving bonds" (*ST,* 268), stronger than all other forces on earth, even the High Magic, and where he may be able to help others. Merriman reminds him of the consequences of such a choice: He will be mortal and not remember what has passed here. Arthur, like the best fathers of all times and places, tells Bran to go where he feels he should go, " 'and my blessing go with you' " (*ST,* 269). He steps out onto land, and Bran runs to embrace him; then he hands the sword to his father, before the ship, with Arthur once more aboard, sails over the sky.

Here we are for the last time, Merriman tells the children, in the place that we were destined to be. He tells them to look hard and keep some of what they see alive. (This is the place where Will saw—through the outline of swans—men centuries before, hiding their chalices and jewels from the Dark.) The story has come full circle back to the Chiltern Hills beyond the Thames Valley of Buckinghamshire.

Then the time changes (the final time-slip). The air dances, the colors darken, different shapes rise in the distance. The children stand "quiet as standing stones" (*ST,* 272), as Merriman takes his leave, telling them that this is their world now; it has been delivered, with their help, by the Light, and it is in their hands to preserve things now that men can destroy the world if they do not control the evil that is inside them.

The last words to him are Simon's: they will try their best (Simon is the one closest in age to adulthood; his responsibility for taking leadership in the human world is now the most imminent). Then the last magic occurs. Because all of these children, except for Will, are mortal and cannot think as Old Ones, Merriman explains, what they have learned about the Old Ones or about this quest will be hidden away deep in their minds, and they will remember it only in dreams. Be proud of yourselves, he tells them, as he turns to make his way up the mountain, the final raising of his arm becoming the image that will fill their unconscious memories from that time on.

In taking this path, in erasing the children's memories on an unconscious level, Cooper leaves the children's experience intact on an intuitive level. Since this is something of a Jungian notion of how we as a human species operate, it is not an unimportant "place" for their memories to rest. Cooper's own belief about how she herself operates as a writer, very much on an unconscious level, helps us to realize just how significant she considers this level of human consciousness to be. Her narrative choices, as she attests, are often rooted in dreams and intuitions.

Left on this hill of modern times, the children look down at the valley and sea, speaking not of Merriman but merely of the view. Bran is puzzled by a small, colored stone that turns up in his pocket, the one given to him by Gwion in the Lost Land, and he offers it to Jane. Barney hears music. "I think it's time we were starting out," Will said. " 'We've got a long way to go' " (*ST,* 274). Fortunately, they cannot know just *how* far, how difficult, frightening, or formidable will be the way as they move forward (or "back") into their own world—and time.

Thus ends the *Dark Is Rising* sequence as it appears to us today. In the next chapter we will be looking at these books in terms of reader reception, from the time of its publication in the 1970s to the present.

Chapter Five

The *Dark Is Rising* Sequence and Readers

If we step back to examine the reception of the *Dark Is Rising* sequence throughout the 1970s, as the books were emerging, we note an interesting collection of responses: awe, anticipation for the next book, puzzlement, questions, accolades, awards, and—at times—reservations.

There were those who found her child characters in *Over Sea, Under Stone* too cautious and proper,[1] who said the morality in *The Dark Is Rising* was "indefinite" and "motiveless,"[2] and who felt that Will was not a crucial character in *Greenwitch*.[3] Some also pronounced the role of the Light as banal in each of the books because Cooper placed her enchanted world within the real one,[4] and others felt that the Dark and the Light remained "ultimately stereotyped" in *Silver on the Tree*.[5]

For the most part, however, Cooper's works received high praise and enormous respect. Cooper was most often commended for her expertise in storytelling, her ability to draw upon an overwhelming compendium of source material, her eloquent and powerful use of language, and her many spellbinding scenes of terror and poetic beauty. She was at the top of her field with a Newbery Honor Award in 1974 for *The Dark Is Rising* and the Newbery itself in 1976 for *The Grey King*.

In the 1980s and 1990s, readers have tended to study the sequence in areas such as fantasy and folklore rather than assess it, although female critics have complained about Cooper's male characters playing a more active role in the books,[6] and male critics have disagreed with Cooper's decision to erase the children's conscious memory of their adventures at the end of the quest.[7]

Children, for their part, have continued to be avid readers of the books. It is to these two audiences (children and adults) that we turn now. If we consider that the initial audience of any children's book consists of the adults writing, editing, publishing, reviewing, and critiquing a book, we must begin with adults reading as critics before we move on to children, the supposed primary audience of these books.

Adults Reading as Critics

The critical stance is one of intellectual inquiry. Adults are reading—and writing—in their own interests as members of a field. And if that field is children's literature, they see a children's book simply as literature, and they read and write about it as such. Children's books, Canadian critic Lillian Smith has said, "must be subjected to the same standards of criticism as any other form of literature" (quoted by Cooper, *DW,* 21). This is the traditional stance of children's literature criticism: standards, choosing the best (since a good book shapes the mind and heart of young readers). How do we choose the best? What makes a children's book good? In John Rowe Townsend's words, the book has "engaged the whole heart and skill of writers and artists."[8] It has artistic integrity, or, in Sheila Egoff's words, the book is "central to a cultural heritage"; it presents "the coherent and unifying power of human sympathy in vivid images."[9]

Townsend, Smith and Egoff represent the literary critic as liberal humanist, a tradition that Ann Swinfen finds expressed by so many writers of modern fantasy. The writer, Swinfen says, feels a "need to break free [from the dissatisfaction of modern life] and realize full human potential."[10] So canonicity is often the first item of discussion. Is the book distinguished by aesthetic qualities? Has it made a significant contribution to the field? (Has it produced something new and different—a breakthrough, a milestone, a new genre or way of conceiving genre, a fresh and authentic vision of the world?) Is the book generating critical attention—literary analysis, interpretation, new theories?

Traditional Criticism

A book usually becomes a classic—or worthy of the canon—if it has such literary strengths as evocation of scene, depth of character, empathetic characters, original point of view or vision of the world, emotional resonance, experiments with language, and focus in design and structure. In the *Dark Is Rising* sequence, each book has particular strength in at least one of these categories.

The Dark Is Rising sets forth the author's original point of view so completely she never has to explore it as extensively after that. Depth of character is achieved most completely in *The Grey King,* since Cooper allows Will and Bran to work out the quest themselves with no help from Merriman this time, and their inner feelings evolve more visibly. As a result, they probably become her most empathetic characters. Bran may be her most original and therefore most interesting character. Emotional resonance is strongest in *Greenwitch,* since the dynamic of the painter and the Greenwitch is stronger than any conflicts among human characters in the cast; each is an emotional "giant" in this war of human and superhuman emotions. *Silver on the Tree* has the most memorable experiments with language in terms of pictorial scenes; therefore, it is also strongest in evocation of scene, although *Over Sea, Under Stone* is especially strong in the category of scene building.

The Grey King has the most effective focus in structural pattern and pacing. There are neither superfluous characters nor scenes, as we see in *Silver on the Tree,* in which there is an overburdened plot and many dispensable scenes, since characters featured in those scenes, namely Blodwen Rowlands and Caradog Lewis, cannot, in the space allotted to them in this already bulging design, become fully developed characters with plausible motivation for their behavior.

At times Cooper has been the toughest traditional critic of her own books, remarking that *Silver on the Tree* "suffered from being the last book" (*DW,* 195) of the sequence, when she was tying up all the loose ends: "It had too much in it. My head was going off in all directions. Its structure is not terrific" (*DW,* 195). No one excels at evoking scene better than Cooper, however, and that is why *Silver on the Tree* is such a satisfying book despite the structural problems. Her blending of genres in the four fantasy books of the sequence produces something new and original; for those fascinated with time-slip fantasy as a genre, her fusion of legendary pictures released into shifting scenes of time is important and exciting.

She incorporates many actual instances of the Dark in action; thus, John Rowe Townsend's remark that "it is difficult to work out just what the Dark is, what it intends to do and what it actually *does,* other than create scenic and atmospheric effects" (Townsend, 223) is puzzling. First and foremost, there are the greedy usurpers—Saxons, Danes, Romans—who invade Britain century after century, displacing the Celts and driving them farther and farther to the west. All of these are echoed by modern-day tyrants like the Nazi paratrooper of Cooper's childhood nighttime imaginings, who lurk in the pages of these books.

Various institutions—religion, medicine, education—do not emerge unscathed. Hastings of *Over Sea, Under Stone* pretends to be a vicar. Dr. Armstrong of *The Dark Is Rising* suppresses the Walker's wild rambling with injections of drugs. Thus she focuses on medical ethics and the "strong-arming" of any who break the norms and are consequently silenced, controlled, or changed. The three interrogators that Bran and Will meet in the cavern of Bird Rock in *The Grey King* (Arthur, Merlin, and the Lord of the Dark) utilize one of the most banal teaching strategies: rote memorization for testing students, illustrating the dogmatic transmission of facts that so often stultifies true learning. However, what Cooper depicts is also authentic pedagogy for the fifth century, in which the historical Arthur might have lived. (Describing educational principles of the Romans, Ashe says they valued the "training of the intellect" more than "the intellect itself" [Ashe, 34] and "authority more than originality" [Ashe, 65]).

Cooper's vision of the world is certainly unique. The question that arises, however, is how well does her created world succeed with critics? The answer will depend, of course, on what particular critical theory is brought to bear on the text.

Critical Theories

Recent discussions of Cooper's work have utilized genre theory, cultural studies, reader-response theory, as well as interdisciplinary approaches involving folklore, feminist criticism, and psychology.

Sheila Egoff, Ann Swinfen, C. W. Sullivan, and Charlotte Spivack have studied the *Dark Is Rising* sequence as fantasy, but each has proceeded very differently. Egoff utilizes traditional literary criticism; Swinfen's interest is social criticism; Sullivan traces the use of Celtic folklore in selected fantasies, and Spivack is attempting to revise the canon in terms of greater respect for fantasy—and for female fantasy writers in particular.

From a liberal humanist perspective in *Worlds Within,* Egoff studies the history of children's literature in terms of fantasy, dividing the genre into nine subgenres. She places Cooper into that of epic fantasy, a category she identifies as having three dominant traits: a close connection to the oral tradition of legend, a continuous conflict of good and evil, and the hero doing battle "for the common good."[11] Moreover, she compartmentalizes her subgenres of fantasy to such an extent that categories of epic fantasy and what she describes as past-time fantasy never blend the way they do in Cooper's work.

Swinfen, on the other hand, studies fantasy in order to see what it tries to achieve in terms of contemporary history and the individual.

Unlike Egoff, Swinfen discusses Cooper in terms of the parallel worlds of time (past and present operating together at once) that she creates. Thus, she can posit as a theory that *The Dark Is Rising* "uses many time shifts to explore the fundamental unity in human affairs" (Swinfen, 55), although she adds that this parallelism of then and now is not Cooper's primary concern for the sequence as a whole.

Sullivan employs what he calls "myth-in-literature criticism" (150) in order to study how authors of High Fantasy utilize Celtic sources, which, he feels, help "promote an affective sense of the impossible as perhaps no other setting with a real-world cognate would" (94). Celtic materials, he notes, "long associated with magic and mystery," (94) increase a sense of "cognitive impossibility" (88) or wonder; they increase the "imaginative vision" (150) of the work; they also clarify moral issues at stake for the hero (the larger-than-life, Good-versus-Evil conflict or theme).

Spivack's study of fantasy novels by women causes her to notice a "conventional" male role of warrior (aggressive, courageous, strong) with a goal of dominating others or achieving power. This portrayal is rejected by female authors for both their male and female characters. Female authors produce protagonists that are strong and courageous, yet sensitive or intuitive, with de-emphasized power. Female protagonists are especially committed to "self-fulfillment and protection of the community" (8) and the developing of human relationships in lieu of confrontational battles.

Spivack notes that Jane is the sensitive, intuitive sibling who plays a significant role in both *Greenwitch* and *Silver on the Tree,* but she does so through "communication rather than action" (43), thus developing a relational connection both to the Greenwitch and the Lady rather than undergoing the actual, physical journey to the Lost Land that Will and Bran make. She remarks that Cooper emphasizes the sensitive and intuitive traits of these two male characters, a role that contrasts with the usual emphasis on heroes doing battle to win a quest.

What Spivack may be overlooking, however, is that developing and maintaining a relationship is a way of action for Jane, although a less unconventional one. Her discussion also illustrates how conventional most feminist criticism has been in relation to children's books, since it rarely goes beyond advocating that females take on conventional male roles: physical action and aggressiveness rather than passive behavior. (Doing what the boys do becomes the be-all and end-all for a self-actualizing female character.)

If we look at the book, in terms of cultural history, we see that Jane, as shaman time-traveler in *Greenwitch,* is not a conventional female; the Greenwitch is not a conventional fertility symbol, and the Lady who seems to be the epitome of the medieval romantic heroine may be something else, too. It is surprising that Spivack, who finds Cooper's series "outstanding for its integral use of Celtic myth and legend" (49), does not notice that the Lady of *The Dark Is Rising* and *Silver on the Tree;* Tethys of *Greenwitch;* Gwen of *The Grey King;* and Jane produce a quartet of Celtic females who represent the gradual suppression of female independence from early Celtic society to the present day.

Thus, Cooper's allusion to the Hunting of the Wren in connection to the Lady in *The Dark Is Rising.* Females have been hunted (oppressed, beleaguered, put to death) since the time when patriarchy superseded matriarchy in Celtic cultures, Cooper implies, when she links the Lady and wren; consequently, we have the delicate, fragile condition of the Lady, now in her centuries-old condition, and the fact that her strength is fading to the extent that she rests on the bier with the hunted wren.

Celtic pagan people evolved from "Danu, the mother goddess" (Ellis 1996, 10), from the Danube River, where the Celts were thought to have developed their earliest society; the Lady functions well in this same role, or as all women combined. Known by many names, she is woman of all times or all women of Time. But the "supreme feminine symbol" was the sea filled with strange creatures like the *afanc* and with hidden treasures that "faultless heroes" (Ellis, 1996, 25) were allowed to find in the old myths. As patriarchal ideas began to replace matriarchal ones, however, the sea as a dangerous and forbidden place attained more emphasis in stories. The sea as mother of life took on the same secret, dangerous, and forbidden aspects that we see dramatized in *Greenwitch.*

A famous Celtic woman of myth, Ellis observes, was Gwenhwyfar, wife of the Celtic warrior Arthur in the fifth-century legendary histories. Before Christian motifs in medieval romance began filtering through the stories, Gwenhwyfar was not the oppressed Gwen that Cooper chose to incorporate into *The Grey King.* This later Guinevere, based on medieval, Anglo-Norman lore, was sent to a nunnery for her independence and sexuality (the influence of patriarchal Christianity). But in her own pre-Christian Celtic day, before the Roman image of Mary "turned into a positive barrier to feminine fulfillment" (Ellis 1996, 38), her sexual relationships would have carried neither guilt nor disgrace. (Notice Gwen of *The Grey King* and her bowed head returning to the nunnery with Merriman, having given up her son, Bran.)

In an earlier time, Gwenhwyfar lived in harmony, equity, and social partnership with men. "Women had a position in early Celtic society," says Ellis. "They were able to govern; they played an active part in political, social and religious life. They could be warriors, doctors, physicians, judges and poets. They could own property and they remained the owner of that property even when married. They could freely choose their partners, they could divorce, and if they were deserted, molested or maltreated then they had the right to claim considerable damages" (Ellis 1996, 267).

The Lady in the *Dark Is Rising* sequence plays this part well. In *The Dark Is Rising,* she sits with Merriman in the Great Hall in what Ellis would describe as "comfortable equality which does not rely on the superiority of one sex over another" (Ellis 1996, 268). When Will enters this past time to learn who he is, she helps to instruct him. In *Silver on the Tree,* she is considered the "last height of power" (*ST,* 169) among the Old Ones. Certainly this is a matriarchal world when she can be so described. Here in this book, she also serves as negotiator in the dispute about Bran's right to Arthur's sword, and she decides for John Rowlands whether he is to remember his wife's transgression (she makes the ruling judgment). She arrives and leaves with Arthur at the battle of Badon scenes, and she stands as his equal. Whenever she appears with either Merriman or Arthur, there is always the appearance of comfortable equality between them, the "casual closeness" of family (*ST,* 265).

So we see two "Guineveres" in the *Dark Is Rising* sequence, the one of early Celts, called the Lady, and the one of medieval Arthurian romance, called Gwen. It is the Lady who appears to Jane in the "singing" mountains of Wales in *Silver on the Tree* because like must communicate to like. And they are alike in that they are both females who can use their constructive and creative powers to carry out important tasks for their people in the same way that women of early Celtic society functioned.

The Lady calls Jane "Juno" (*Silver on the Tree,* 90), for, like Juno, the Roman queen of the gods, Gwenhwyfar was a leader of her own Celtic people, an independent, resourceful woman of courage. Like them both, the Lady comes bearing the message for Jane, as well as inspiring her to have courage as she goes forward in the quest. Jane needs this inspiration; she is very much the protected—and therefore frightened—female of post-Celtic, patriarchal Christian days, whose most courageous and creative acts must often be suppressed, subverted, sublimated, and relegated to the subconscious or the Jungian anima.

The psychic wholeness that Cooper's females achieve with their creative power speaks easily to Jungian theories of individuation. Tethys in her female power, Jane as shaman time-traveler, even Gwen with her personal sacrifices, all attain some degree of integrated selfhood. The Lady becomes, in Jungian terms, a "single, homogeneous being" (Jung, 395), embracing all females: all "Gwen" figures of legend, including especially Gwenhwyfar, the Mother Goddess and the young girl of modern days. She is truly a "Queen of every hive" (*ST,* 169) and the only woman of significance to be seen in part 3 of *Silver on the Tree,* called "The Lost Land." So strong is her presence that she appears through her physical absence: She is seen only in a picture that Will and Bran discover in the library of the king's palace.

But before this scene, there is another Jungian one: Will and Bran stand on a golden roof overlooking the City of the Lost Land. This roof represents an image similar to the tower that Jung built as an upper story to the Bollingen house on his own land and that later came to signify for him "an extension of consciousness" (Jung, 225) or a "place of spiritual concentration" (Jung, 224):

> From the beginning I felt the Tower as in some way a place of maturation— a maternal womb or a maternal figure in which I could become what I was, what I am and will be. It gave me a feeling as if I were being reborn in stone. It is thus a concretization of the individuation process . . . It might also be said that I built it in a kind of dream. Only afterward did I see how all the parts fitted together and that a meaningful form had resulted: a symbol of psychic wholeness. (Jung, 225)

The study of Jungian theories could easily be applied to the numerous remarks Cooper has made about the way her own dreams were employed in *Silver on the Tree.* As she commented in 1980: "Out of that part of the mind that is not sleeping, there can come an image so powerful that it is an experience—odd and meaningless in itself, but always leaving a very strong visual impression and a sensation of intense joy. I had one of those dreams three of four years ago" (*DW,* 38). She was standing high on a bridge in a city (as were Will and Bran); she woke with a feeling of wonder and excitement and was able to transfer that feeling (the *frisson*) to the children of *Silver on the Tree.*

Another dream used in that book was the recurrent one she had about a "strange library-theater" (*DW,* 58). But the dream stopped occurring when she included it her writing. "Perhaps it wanted a life of its own," she says, "a chance to get into other imaginations than mine, and was now content that it had been set free" (*DW,* 58). She then goes on to relate the dream to her own life, saying that just as she was finishing *Silver on the Tree,* she was beginning to write for the theater. And she has been moving between the two settings ever since: "Fantasy tells me where I am" (*DW,* 61), concluded Cooper.

There is a mystical, intuitive side to Cooper that emerges in many of the statements she makes about her choice of genre and the way her imagination works. There is an equally rational, perceptual side that we see when she discusses the war of her childhood and the way it influenced her work. This latter aspect leads to cultural and personal history as another approach to the study of her work. (We understand England of the 1940s better from not only *Dawn of Fear* but also the *Dark Is Rising* sequence. And we understand the sequence better after hearing about the war years of her childhood.)

Cooper tells us that the scene of Will's attic bedroom, when a rook beats down upon the skylight in *The Dark Is Rising,* arose from her fear of the German planes that her father faced as a sergeant in the Home Guard. The entire idea of the Dark and the Light, the ancient conflict of good and evil, she says, has its "deepest roots" (*DW,* 146) in this war. "Night is dark and cold . . . Down in the air-raid shelter at the age of six . . . night was dangerous" (*DW,* 146). She does not say the rooks who attack the church on Christmas Day in this book (the "black flurries of malevolence, cawing and croaking" [*DR,* 127] that come swooping up and shrieking) are related to the German V-1s, "the fast, pilotless planes filled with explosives, sent off with just enough fuel in their tanks to reach the South of England" (*DW,* 142). But we surmise that they are, at least at a subconscious level, linked one to the other.

Yet the "searing brilliance" (*DW,* 147) of the atomic bomb dropped on Hiroshima to end the war was just as dangerous, she explains. "In war, the Dark and the Light inevitably behave very much alike" (*DW,* 150), she adds, noting the significance of the Dark Riders (at the end of *Silver on the Tree),* who wear robes of both black and white. Absolutes, extremists, bullies of either side, and impossible ideals are "doomed to be always destructive, always cruel" (*DW,* 151). The rooks, in fact, always arrive in the snow.

Elizabeth Baer feels that World War II has caused a difference in the way we would think about using the Arthurian legends in children's literature and that the Holocaust, in particular, changed the way Cooper would have used them. Now adults have a "more horrific concept of evil,"[12] Baer asserts and because of this, "there is an obligation to explore that condition in literature for children in order to warn children about evil in the world around them" (Baer, 83). But the question arises, should children's literature serve the didactic purpose that Baer says it has had for its long history? The critic who says yes has crossed into a different role, that of caretaker.

Whereas critics read and write primarily in their own interests as members of a discipline, field, or other adult endeavor, caretakers (or caretaker-critics) are reading and writing in what they perceive to be children's interests. Caretakers are more likely to discuss children's books in terms of issues—moral, social, cultural, political—that they assume will affect children when they read. They are often guided by social issues involving gender, class, race, and culture (censorship, gender bias, authenticity of authorship, misunderstandings of cultural beliefs and values, cultural inequities).

Cooper remembers that the *Dark Is Rising* sequence was attacked by the Council for Inter-Racial Relations for its metaphysical configuration of Light and Dark/Good and Evil. But as she explains, the "deepest roots" of her books are "embedded in war" (*DW,* 146), and they reach down to primitive man (of whatever color) and her own memories of war when night was dangerous and dark in the air-raid shelter.

These books, she relates, were also attacked by the Church of Scotland's Board of Social Responsibility for "undermining the Christian faith"; but she again traces their ethical underpinning not to any "theistic ideal" (*DW,* 150) but instead to her own memories as a wartime child observing man's inhumanity to man. Her war novel, *Dawn of Fear,* is an important introduction or companion piece to the sequence. Baer suggests that *Dawn of Fear* should, in fact, be read as part of the series, as a "gloss" or "subtext" of it, since it also focuses on war and the duality of human nature.

Traditional critics, critical theorists, and caretaker-critics all reveal the loftiest motives of adults working with books marketed for children. But what do these motives really have to do with actual children, like the 12-year-old who wrote Cooper to say, " 'Your books seem to fit me just right' " (*DW,* 63)? Adults reading as critics rarely conduct the painstaking, time-consuming work of ethnographic and case-study research, eliciting and recording children's responses. Instead, they often wave aside the value of such work with the comment, "Which child?" as if the responses of child readers would be too varied to be informative.

But if it is true that children's books are really—and primarily—for children (the "proper readers" of such books, as Cooper says, [*DW,* 120]), then one child, or any child, is of the greatest importance to an intellectual inquiry we bring to bear on children's books.

Child Readers

"I read the whole sequence in sixth grade," Derek, age 15, told me the day I invited him to talk about his memories of the *Dark Is Rising* sequence. "They came in one collection. I read *Over Sea, Under Stone* and really liked that one, and it was the prelude to the whole series. So I just continued reading them. It was difficult for me to read the books. I thought she was a really advanced writer. I understood them; they were just a little more advanced, compared to what I had been reading."

I wanted to learn from Derek which book he had liked best at that time in order to understand better what a children's book is and what these books might tell us about a child's preoccupations, or how children might read differently from adults. "I liked *Greenwitch* the best," Derek replied. "It took place on the sea near Cornwall. It took place in the summer. I like books that take place near water in the summer. Those are my favorite kinds."

I asked him what he remembered about *Greenwitch,* and he continued: "There's this other kid, these brothers and sisters, from *Over Sea, Under Stone.* And in *The Dark Is Rising,* there's this other boy introduced, and then in *Greenwitch,* this boy joins the brothers and sister in Cornwall. I remember they both were sort of unsure why the others were there. They thought they were the only ones who knew about it and at first they didn't want to do anything together, but they came to like each other later. And I remember the Greenwitch festival that took place. They made it out of sticks and seaweed, I remember that. It seemed real, a ritual or festival that would have taken place years ago and they carried the tradition on."

I asked if he remembered the scene that began with Jane jumping off into the water, flying into it, and then later, waking up and thinking it was a dream. I wanted to know if he thought this really was a dream or if she actually went down under the water where the Greenwitch was. "It's coming back," he replied. "I imagined her going underwater actually." Then I mentioned the scene in which Merriman and Will flew down into the water, like birds and whether or not he thought it was real. He said, "Since that was a magical fantasy type of thing going on, I thought that was true or as real as you could get."

Derek's responses show us how easily children adapt to genre, rather than intellectualizing about it as adults tend to do. The scene of Jane underwater was one that had left me uncertain as to whether it were to be interpreted as "real" within the context of the fantasy. At first I assumed it was a dream, but the placement of the scene *before* the scene of Jane waking up in her bedroom caused me to think Cooper wanted the "reality" left ambiguous. Yet all adult critics I have read consider this entire scene-cluster as a dream, just as Jane later believes it to be (or as Merriman wants her to believe, if he has erased the "magic" of it from her memory).

Derek's comments also tell us a great deal about what out-of-school pleasure reading is for children: the water, the summer setting, an interest in the children's relationships with one another. When Derek talks about other books he is currently reading, we begin to see even more about why there was (and is) for him this importance regarding peer relationships.

"I like reading books about kids around my own age," Derek said. "My favorite types of books, like *Huckleberry Finn* and *Tom Sawyer,* are about kids who are close to my age. I can relate better to them, even if the things they do aren't what I do. I read all of Twain's books two summers ago. Last summer I read *Hamlet* on my own, because I went to see a play in Stratford, Ontario, with my grandparents. I've read a lot of Stephen King; I like those. Right now I'm reading John Irving's *Cider House Rules.* I started a book by John Updike, *Rabbit Run,* but it was depressing, so I quit reading it, because I read really just to be happy. If the story makes me happy, [I would not stop reading it], even if it's a depressing subject, 'cause some writers make a depressing subject happy. But this story was really depressing. It depends on how the author handles it."

The many readers (children, young adults, even adults looking back at themselves at younger ages) who have written to Cooper sharing their feelings about her fantasy sequence, produce testimony that an author can take a threatening subject (the constant battle of the Dark to overtake the Light) and make it "happier." How do they say she does it? Through the "realism" of fantasy, it seems.

For a British 13-year-old, one who relished adventure, the ability to slip out of "this world and into another" (*DW,* 63) was the key. Reading about the Old Ones fighting the Dark caused an American 13-year-old from Texas to wish to be in that other world, "protecting mankind from harm" (*DW,* 63). This desire or need to do or save something, the struggle that stands at the heart of these books, seems to reach the children who become the most strongly engaged. " 'You give all of us the chance to leave the mundane struggles we face and enter a slightly grander struggle for a while' " (*DW,* 63), a reader of age 21 wrote to Cooper. Another reader, a 16-year-old from Sweden, spoke of the strong feeling the books released, of wanting " 'to climb up to the pages and walk straight into it and help Will and his friends' " (*DW,* 63).

Then there is, beyond this sense of adventure and participation in a high quest or struggle, the insight into self that must be every writer's ultimate vision. As a 15-year-old girl wrote to say, the books " 'have helped me to see the good and evil in myself' " (*DW,* 136). That letter, states Cooper, has haunted her ever since. "I often wonder what has become of her" (*DW,* 136), she says. When a very deep involvement with a book develops for a child, reading becomes a different kind of experience. The place of the book in a child's life is very significant indeed if the child feels compelled to communicate with an author (especially in cases like these, when the readers are not compelled by a classroom activity to do so).

Listening to children and young adults talk about the *Dark Is Rising* sequence, we begin to sense links among readers, no matter how far apart they are in nationality, region, gender, age, or degree of reading experience. What seems similar in these responses, especially those of Derek and the children who wrote letters to Cooper, is the social aspect of reading. There is the desire for adventure, yes, but beyond this, these young readers speak of bonds they have forged with Cooper's characters, the same "loving bonds" that Cooper is setting forth throughout the sequence. As Merriman explains at the end of the sequence, the ability to form loving bonds is the one feature that humans have in common with one another and that sets them off from those of the High Magic who live for principles or immutable rules rather than in the "light" of human frailties, propensities, or preoccupations.

It is the human element that these young readers emphasize, too. Derek remembered that the Drew children eventually came to like one another later, and a 16-year-old from Sweden wanted to walk right into the books "to help Will and his friends." These children were not using literature merely to decipher the world; nor were they merely using the world to read literature. They were reading literature *as* the world, particularly their own world in terms of the importance they, in their own child world, held for peer friendships.

The least "happy" book of the sequence, in terms of peer friendships, is *The Dark Is Rising*. As the book opens, Will is alone almost immediately, beset with learning about his heritage as an Old One and confined most often to the company of Merriman, the Lady, Hawkin, other Old Ones, or the Dark Rider. It is a cold atmosphere, filled with very few warm social scenes or feelings. Yet, as Derek found, either Cooper managed to make these "depressing" scenes "happy" or she made the unhappy aspects realistic to *him*.

It is as individuals reading in very unique and personal ways that children and young adults like Derek help us to see another audience of children's books. Do adults read children's books in the same way at times, not primarily or directly for their work in a particular discipline or field, but simply and *really* for pleasure, or as Derek says, "really just to be happy"?

Adults Reading for Pleasure

Why would adults read children's books if they were not being paid or pressed to do so? Or would they? Do adults ever come into contact with children's literature in an entirely separate context from actual or theoretical children and take just as much pleasure from the books as children? Who knows how the actress Jessica Tandy encountered *The Dark Is Rising*, but as Cooper tells the story, she already knew about Cooper and her books and had been trying to get her husband, Hume Cronyn, to read them long before Cooper met this famous couple. Later Cooper says she discovered that Jessica Tandy "loved being given authors she hadn't yet discovered, and I loved giving her them: Lucy Boston, Penelope Lively, Philippa Pearce, Patricia Wrightson, Betty Levin, Nina Bawden, and on, and on" (*DW,* 4). As for why Tandy enjoyed these books, Cooper explains it best: "Many things change as we grow up . . . but a few do not, and one of them is the imagination" (*DW,* 122).

Cooper in fact reverses the thinking of what is children's literature when she speaks of "the freshness of a child's vision of the world" that "every artist strives to retain" (*DW,* 40–41), and it would, in fact, produce reader appeal at any age. The book would be as Derek has described—"happy"—the writer having made any "unhappy" aspects realistic enough that the reader becomes engaged by the power of the scene. How does Cooper achieve such a feat? What makes her such a master of the evocative scene?

Any one of these books of the *Dark Is Rising* sequence shows us, but *Silver in the Tree* may be the "happiest" book of all. From the standpoint of an adult reading simply for pleasure, there is so much of the book to read and so much of it is *good*. Thus the best way to write about it may be in terms of "personal" rather than "traditional" criticism, a category that has recently reemerged as a legitimate way of writing about literature. It is also a way that adults reading children's books for no other reason than their own pleasure may find particularly useful, not only because it brings them closer to the way children read but also because intellectual inquiry need not begin or end with traditional criticism.

Personal Criticism

At the same time, traditional criticism does not, of course, preclude pleasure as part of the reading process. The pleasure is simply expressed differently. Criticism, at least in academe, has most often been formulated in terms of objective, universal thinking, with reason (implying an impersonal, distanced, neutral voice) as opposed to emotion, impressions, intuitions, subjectivity) as the order of the day. How did it all begin in this era, this penchant for the impersonal, when only a century before, in the essays that commanded intellectual inquiry in literary circles, personal taste, elegance, and discrimination produced the only necessary authority for readers?

"Perhaps," says Norman Holland, one of the participants of a Modern Language Association Forum in 1995, on the place of the personal in scholarship, "we needed to make literary studies respectable, objective, and scientific. We were to make " 'a contribution to knowledge' "[13] and that meant making "the self less visible" ("Forum," 1147). But as he continues, "The self permeates reading. The self therefore permeates criticism, theory, and scholarship" ("Forum," 1146), and "[i]n this postmodern age, we are rightly sceptical about claims to objectivity" ("Forum," 1146). Karl Kroeber, another participant, marks the origin of the critic's shift from *we* to *I* as a time in the 1970s when critics in academe "lost any sense of participating" in a "meaningfully shared professional enterprise" ("Forum," 1163). Most would attribute it to a more recent era, when the rise of cultural critics sounded a note for calling many different voices out of silence.

Mary Ann Caws calls for a "conversational criticism" in which the personal includes and dialogues with the other (the traditional mode) evolving "its own kind of knowledge" (1160), as it goes along. It is with

Caws that we might wish to pause and turn back to Cooper's work, for in doing so, we may see personal criticism intersecting with reader-response studies. Traditional criticism does not have to be discarded when we make a place for the personal in our scholarship; the personal can travel along easily beside the impersonal, with the goal of each being the same: to help readers better understand a book and its author in terms of what happens when we ourselves enter the text, observing and noticing our own reception of it. Or as Richard Flores has observed, "In writing myself into my work, I do not pretend to speak for all but try to write from a place worth noting and knowing" ("Forum," 1166).

Personal Criticism and *Silver on the Tree*

We have already seen what happens from the standpoint of traditional criticism when we discuss *Silver on the Tree*. We get caught up in notions of structure and tend to lose sight of what makes literature, and this book in particular, so pleasurable: evocation of scene. To me, what makes this book remarkable is the lyrical poetry of Cooper's scene building, the way she uses imagery of every possible sense impression to stop the action and build meaning, mood, and myth making through word pictures.

Each composite picture is a small story of its own, an inner story within the main story, a distillation of experience operating very much like a dream (it means something that seems just right; at the same time it leaves the dreamer unable to consciously grasp just what the something is). The pictures reveal meaning without ever stating it; thus, we move through the book with tacit knowing, alongside the characters.

When Will watches his brother Stephen threading his fishing rod, a swan swims past "clearly through the outline of Stephen's body" (*ST,* 3) rather than behind him. Then, through the swan's outline, Will sees another scene (a visual framing device), an ancient grassy slope filled with people of the Bronze Age in this same part of the Thames Valley, who are running away from foreign invaders. The swan scene is a pictorial time-slip, producing a story of how Will enters another dimension of time. We are not told how it happens; it is simply shown to us through Will's eyes in this small "moving" picture.

This book is also filled with numerous metaphorical "stills." One of the earliest ones is the picture Cooper creates of the plume moths. Here two similes are used to double and then triple the picture, another nesting-box image that arises when the simile unfolds into a cluster of metaphors. The tiny white plume moths flurry around Stephen so that he forgets what Will has told him about the quest of the Old Ones. They are "like infinitely small birds fashioned of snowflakes; silent, ghostly, each tiny wing a filigree of five delicate feathers, all white" (*ST,* 14). The moths are like birds; the birds are like snowflakes; the snowflakes are ghosts—or ghostly—each wing is like a snowflake (white, delicate, and feathered—like a bird).

Sometimes these "stills" are sight-and-sound pictures, like the one she creates of the music of the Old Ones that "fell through the air like sunlight" (*ST,* 93). Sometimes they are sight-and-touch images, like her description of the Sign of water that Will has retrieved from the excavation in Rome: "clear crystal, engraved with delicate symbols and patterns like a circle of snowflakes caught in ice" (*ST,* 33). And sometimes the images, filled with emotional resonance, produce a perfect stillness through the echoes of song, when sound, color, and the gentlest of motion brings the Lady floating into sight in a fragile, rose-colored "brightness" (*ST,* 90).

Another scene of motion, this time of rolling movement, is that of the sea at low tide in Dyfi estuary, when the waves fall back; trees, buildings, and an entire city suddenly spring up, and the children glimpse "a pencil of light standing, a faraway tower gleaming like white fire" (*ST,* 104). This scene is the prelude to a rich inner story (the journey of Will and Bran to the Lost Land and back again) that unfolds scene by scene. It progresses from the library-theater setting of Cooper's remembered dream to the maze of mirrors and the glass tower where they find the king and the crystal sword, followed by the storm that crashes upon the Lost Land, sending it back down into the sea.

The crescendo of words rises like the storm, the music of Gwion's harp echoing in the rhythm of the passage: "Sea grew dark as sky; there was a new rumbling now . . . and a huge wall of water came thundering toward them from the sea . . . swallowing trees and land and the lines of the river, spreading, swirling, wild . . . But Gwion's music went on. The sea struck at the tower somewhere below; they felt it shake beneath their feet. Wave after wave came roaring, the sea rose higher, the king's light voice called out on the warm fierce wind, 'Lost! Lost!' " (*ST,* 109). Finally Gwion stands beside the fragile king, shouting for Will and Bran to go without him. They refuse; then he explains that he belongs there, the last flash of a smile playing over his "shadowy bearded face" (*ST,* 209).

Silver on the Tree is a rich book that we can read more than once, each time discovering more of these evocative scenes and perhaps even different ones from the previous reading. The library-theater scene may be one of the most arresting on a first reading. It was for me. On my second reading, I was mesmerized by the swans. On my third reading, I was caught up in the waters rising in the Lost Land to the extent that it became a very powerful *frisson,* very unlike my first reading when I raced through this part, scarcely noticing or responding to the strong pathos of Gwion's predicament. It seems to me this is very likely the best scene in the entire sequence, for momentum, pacing, precision of language, emotional resonance, and, most of all, empathetic characters.

The scene is so complete that it unfolds into a story of its own, crystallizing as the heart of Cooper's vision of the world (Gwion makes the ultimate sacrifice of death over life because of loving bonds). This idea, which ultimately emerges in Merriman's words at the end of the book, is what the five children will see and take as their model, and that is why it is here for Bran and Will, the Old One, to experience first. Cooper is able to produce exceptional depth of character for an adult figure with Gwion, and she does so by placing him in only one portion of the entire book and making him a guiding, mediating figure for the children rather than a human in conflict with the Light or the Dark, as Hawkin, Caradog, and the painter were.

Gwion is her most empathetic adult character. Long before he says he will not leave the king and the Lost Land, we know it from his loyal and tender treatment of the king. In a few deft strokes, Cooper produces a small masterpiece in this portrait. We leave Gwion as regretfully as Bran and Will, wishing to see more of him. In fact, this entire book, large with scenes and characters as it is, unwieldy, filled to overflowing, never becomes tiresome or boring. And I find myself at the end of it wishing to read all that Cooper says she had to cut from the book.

Yet like Derek, if I were to choose one book from any of the sequence as my favorite, it would be *Greenwitch.*

Personal Criticism and *Greenwitch*

I like *Greenwitch* for the ideas Cooper chose to weave through the book—that the women of a village would make a nature goddess from tree branches, that this object would come to life because of a child's wish (fierce caring producing out of the Wild Magic, loving bonds), that an obsessed painter would produce an repellent abstract painting and a child would know intuitively what was wrong with it, that two children would discover a magical gypsy caravan, and that the Greenwitch could in its fury fill an entire village with its angry power (I have looked at storms differently after reading this book, "reading" into them a witch's power). Also memorable is the bright, gypsy caravan that could, like Cinderella after midnight, turn into rags and tatters, its colors dull, its paint peeling, its entire being simply an empty shell of its magical, illusory, former "self," a strong parallel to the gypsy culture itself after World War II, when the Nazis obliterated 500,000 gypsies.[14]

I am fascinated and intrigued by all of that, but what especially draws me into the book is the dynamic between Jane and the Greenwitch, the fact that Jane is given a larger, more responsible, part in this book than she had previously in *Over Sea, Under Stone*. Perhaps it is my own female gender that influences my reading, for Derek has given no special attention to Jane. The unit of children is what interests him; he feels Jane is simply one of the unit, and I begin to suspect, from talking with him, that male and female readers may see Cooper's characters differently. (We attend to characters when we find traits like our own in them.)

I was always a fearful child, too, and one, like Jane, who was conscientious, courteous, and thoughtful—or at least, as a female, being reminded constantly to be so. Jane, as a character, does not irritate or even worry me. There are no "shoulds" as I read this book (that Jane should be more adventuresome, more aggressive, more independent). Instead I find that the challenges to which she rises in the face of her fears and shyness is what draws me into the book. When Jane touches the fearful branch of this wild creature, the Greenwitch, and wishes her to be happy, I admire her strong, empathetic insight. This is what I would wish to have been like as a child. Would I have been this mature? This strong and insightful? Probably not; I was the youngest, always protected and indulged; Jane is a middle child; and perhaps she is more empathetic because she has had a great deal of practice in accommodating herself to both an older and a younger sibling.

When Jane leaps into the water from Kemare Head in chapter 4, I relish, in psychic terms, the adventure she has created for herself. She *had* to create this moment not only because males in this "unit" do the running and fighting but also because the immortals do the flying. Jane is not one of the Old Ones, who, like Will and Merriman, have been trained to fly and survive as water creatures. But she is worried about the Greenwitch, and her fierce caring enables her to go where she wants to be. It carries her to a psychic dimension, more powerful even than a physical one, or, to the context of the fantasy, to the actual ocean depths safely—and then back again.

In other words, although human and without supernatural powers, Jane has such strong empathy (perhaps a female "power" or "gift" or the skill of a Celtic shaman) that she can travel like an Old one without being one. But because she is not one of the immortals, she is not able to remember it afterward, as Cooper made clear at the end of *Silver on the Tree*. The mortal children remember their extrahuman adventures only as dreams. And that may be why Jane wakes up from what she perceives is a dream and tells it to Merriman, accepting it as a dream herself.

This scene I find particularly riveting and filled with emotional resonance. Jane can understand the loneliness of the Greenwitch, who is very much a Gollum-like figure from Tolkien, filled with pathos, childish pique, and human petulance. She can also be terrorized by the fury of the Greenwitch, yet still have courage and loyalty. She keeps the conversation going, no matter how threatening the Greenwitch becomes, and promises the Greenwitch she will not tell her secret. She later tells Merriman about their meeting only because she thinks it never really happened.

I particularly like the idea of the Greenwitch figure and the way Cooper has constructed the "making." The idea intrigued me so much on a first reading of the book that I wrote to Susan Cooper, asking her if this were a yearly ritual in Cornwall. Little did I know that some years before this, in 1978, Cooper had addressed the Children's Literature Association, lamenting the fact that so many adults (critics, scholars, teachers, and graduate students writing theses and dissertations) had written to ask for the "specific local and mythical derivations"[15] of the Greenwitch and that Cooper had long since grown annoyed with telling them she had " 'made it all up' " (102).

"Academics long to 'identify' that rite," Cooper wrote back, "but it doesn't exist; it's simply a composite of existing elements that went through the blender of one writer's imagination and came out in a certain form. All fiction is like that, of course; there's no new story under the sun, just the 'cauldron' Professor Tolkien wrote about, into which we all dip. I wonder why people find it so hard to accept that a piece of writing can be vivid, believable and yet not based on fact."[16]

Is it that we want certain things to exist as fact if we find them fascinating? If we discover that a writer made something up, do these things seem not as authentic and real? Or is it that the rite of *The Greenwitch* is surrounded by so much realistic detail that we expect it to be real? There is the reality of dialect spoken by local residents like the Penhallows as well as the reality of streets, harbor, and quay, and of foods, customs, and furnishings of village houses. Because Cooper uses the actual world of Cornwall as the basis for her imagined world, we expect that the rite might have been actual, too. The rite, in fact, achieves so much attention in the story (so many specific details are embedded in Cooper's scenic design for the "making" of the Greenwitch), that it *needs* to accord with the laws of this "actual" Secondary World, as Tolkien explains it.[17] Then the magic spell can remain unbroken.

I suspect that for English readers who know there is no Trewissick, the belief works better. They know there is a St. Austell. They may know that there is a real village in Cornwall five miles from the St. Austell train station where the children disembark in *Over Sea, Under Stone* that is a mirror image of Trewissick. They may even know that there is a real place, Trelissick Gardens, 10 miles southwest of St. Austell that could have inspired Cooper to name her village Trewissick. And so they would know that, once the children step off the real train to St. Austell, Cooper has placed them into her secondary world where standing stones, the village carnival, and sacrifices to the Virgin are all images she has transported across Britain[18] from other times and places to deepen and broaden the Celtic magic.

But Americans, especially adults less familiar with this British "map," assume that everything here is authentic or at least that the Secondary World is a completely authentic place in the real time of now, and they are intrigued by this "real" place. It is not that they disbelieve. The spell has not been broken; Cooper's art has not failed. If anything, it has succeeded only too well for American children who, like Derek, believe in the reality of this setting and for American adults who may study it as "curio," as Tolkien says. "Adults are allowed to collect and study anything, even old theatre programmes or paper bags" (Tolkien, 33), as part of their reading pleasure. The curio reading of adults gives us new images to think with—and about. In fact, the scenes of this book are always so realistic for me that the enjoyment of the reading results, to a great extent, from that creation of place.

As I move along through *Greenwitch,* even now after so many different readings, I believe in the gypsy caravan of this place as real. It is the structure I saw in books as a child and that I now imagine I actually did see. When the Greenwitch enters Jane's mind as the *"poor thing"* who is "always unhappy" (*G,* 108), I marvel at the way Cooper keeps my belief in its actual presence. And the "great mess of little twigs and leaves, hawthorne leaves, and rowan" (*G,* 131) that Mrs. Penhallow finds in Jane's room on the day Jane wakes to find the little silver case does not disturb my belief.

Jane's intelligence is greatly in evidence in the scene of the night before, during which the Greenwitch enters her room and Jane talks to her, asking her about the Wild Magic and its meaning. Never has Jane's composure and reserve, her patience, and her clearly focused personality worked so much to her advantage as it does now when she carefully explains to the Greenwitch why the case is important. Why was Jane given this particular task of the quest? Will is just as composed and empathetic; Simon, just as intelligent; Barney, just as brave and committed to retrieving the manuscript case. Is it simply Jane's gender? Has Cooper chosen a female to lead in this matter because she wanted to show a different kind of female and not simply an unselfish one, since females have certainly seen enough of themselves in literature as the ones who know how to put others first?

Perhaps if Merriman were "using" Jane in this matter as the one who, because of her natural gifts of gender, could most easily complete this mission of retrieving the case from the temperamental Greenwitch, Jane's unselfishness would make her the most *usable* of the children. But Jane is a female who does not think of herself in terms of gender. She does nothing for herself or her gender. She does nothing to prove a girl can do anything a boy can do.

Jane acts simply as one of the unit (the Drew children and Will); she wants—with fierce caring—to help with the quest. She acts simply as a human being who forges loving bonds with others because that is what humans are so capable of doing. And this may be why Derek seemed scarcely to notice Jane in the group or to notice her as a female. She is simply one of them, a friend to the other children and a friend to the Greenwitch. She works hard, in terms of her gifts and abilities, and does the job well. There is a great deal of Cooper in Jane, I suspect, which might in fact help to account for Cooper's success in a man's world in postwar England.

I took a copy of *Greenwitch* with me to England last year, knowing I would be visiting Cornwall. I wanted to see the little seacoast town of Mevagissey (Cooper's Trewissick), and I wanted to browse through the book once more as I traveled down on the train. It was April, the same month that Will and the Drews arrived in Cornwall for the making of the Greenwitch. There was no "making" that I saw, but the village was exactly like the one in Cooper's book; she had been able to produce a perfect likeness of place.

In Mevagissey there are, of course, no standing stones such as those Cooper "transplanted" from places like Avesbury. But the headland looks very much as she described it; the Cornish fishermen dress and speak exactly like her characters, even now, some 30 years later. The main road of the town winds up and around to farms like Pentreath and the church and vicarage that appear in the book.

Most of all I wanted to find the Grey House, where the children went through the wardrobe to find the map, and in a sense I did. Many of the houses were gray; it was simply a matter of choosing the one that seemed just right. I walked the steep little paths that curve up and around the quay on a day that was misty all morning but sun drenched by late afternoon, and I remembered the scene of Simon running from Hastings and the Cornish boy on those same winding paths.

I photographed a man I felt certain was a descendant of King Arthur, and he beamed when I told him. Everyone I met in Mevagissey was decidedly of the Light. Hastings, Withers, Polly, and the painter had not returned, as far as I could tell. Neither had the Greenwitch. It was bitterly cold in Mevagissey, very unlike the April I had envisioned as I read the book. But I found it a happy time.

When I finished rereading *Greenwitch,* I opened a copy of *Over Sea, Under Stone* that I had found in a little secondhand bookshop near Dublin the week before. Earlier it had belonged to Treasa Kelly, age 10. "If lost," she had printed carefully on the inside cover, "please return."

Sitting on a wrought-iron bench around the corner from the road on which Cooper had "painted" the Grey House (she had, in fact, transposed the house from one on Copper Hill Street in Aberdyfi[19]) and not very far from the place that the Greenwitch went to sea and Jane "leaped" down to visit her, I found myself as happily lost in the book as Treasa must have been. I hope that I am "returning" the book in some small way by writing about her in this form of personal reading. To me, Trewissick is a place well worth noting and knowing. And Mevagissey was, too.

Chapter Six
After the *Dark Is Rising* Sequence

Reviewing Susan Cooper's last book of the *Dark Is Rising* sequence in 1977, Penelope Farmer wondered where Cooper could go after such an extraordinary achievement. Perhaps Cooper had told us herself, Farmer decided: "[I]n her book we are told the battleground must shift to the human world" (when Merriman instructs the children that this is "altogether your world now . . . the responsibility and the hope and the promise are in your hands" [*ST*, 272]). Could Cooper then "at last shift her gaze from the complexities of magic to the equally fascinating and not so wholly unrelated complexities of men?" (Farmer, 1409).

To have done so, of course, would have been taking a step backward, for this is what Cooper had already done in *Dawn of Fear*. But she did manage, in her first book after the *Dark Is Rising* sequence, to produce a very real child in terms of emotions, reactions, and cultural beliefs. For the setting of this book, *Jethro and the Jumbie* (1979), she chose the place she visited each summer with her husband and children. Thus her characters were shown speaking the real language of this region as she had listened and mentally recorded it. "Over the years," says Cooper (letter 1985), "I learned (from adults, not children) the local speech patterns, and thought one day that it would be nice if the local kids had something to read that wasn't about foreign white children leading totally different lives in England or the USA."

Reality quickly becomes embedded with magical folk beliefs, since Jethro is a native of the Virgin Islands, where beliefs in the spirits of the dead (the jumbies) are strong. The story also utilizes the magic of dreams to convince Thomas that his younger brother, Jethro, should be taken fishing and that this Jumbie is real, or at least real enough to make Thomas learn to keep his promises. "I knew people who were scared of jumbies (spirits common to most of the Caribbean islands, though less horrific in ours than the zombies of Haitian voodoo)," Cooper goes on to say, "but my own jumbie story was completely made up."

The book is out of print today when so many natives of parallel cultures are telling their own stories and the long picture-book form and use of Caribbean dialect do not work as well with young children learning to read as the simpler picture books that Cooper eventually produced in the early 1990s, *Matthew's Dragon* and *Danny and the Kings*. For the humor, however, the well-told story, the illustrations of Ashley Bryan, and, of course, the jumbie character itself, the book deserves a second look.

Four years after *Jethro and the Jumbie,* it was back to Welsh legend for Cooper. In 1983 she wrote the first of three picture books that reflect her love of the Celtic legends that weave through so many stories like this one she heard as a child. *The Silver Cow* is set in Wales in the same area that Will and Bran discovered in *The Grey King,* the Bearded Lake or Llyn Barfog. The story in many ways echoes that book, since Huw, the young boy, plays the harp just like Bran, and Huw's father, Gwilym Hughes, is as mean spirited as Caradog Prichard, the man who, in the earlier book, wanted to be chosen as Bran's father. Thus the book enables Cooper to tell the story of what it might have been like for Bran if Owen Davies had not been in the picture.

The Silver Cow was followed three years later by *The Selkie Girl,* a retelling of an old legend about the selkies, fairy people who, according to Katherine Briggs, lived on "a dry land under the sea" and who wore "sealskins to move through the water."[1] Once on land, they shed their skins, the male to court mortal women, and the female to be tricked into marrying the man who finds and hides her sealskin. The female never forgot her home in the sea, however, and eventually found a way to return to it because, as an old man in Cooper's version says, "a wild creature will always go back to the wild in the end."[2] The language and narrative flow is particularly effective in Cooper's story. Possessing a strong talent for folktale retellings, Cooper returned to the form once more in 1991, with *Tam Lin,* from the Scottish ballad of the same name.

This story completes her trilogy, illustrated by the noted watercolorist, Warwick Hutton, and is the most provocative of the three, since here, for the first time, Cooper produces a children's book in which the female is strongly adventuresome, bold, and wise: she knows what all true heroes know—there are times when one must break the rules. Margaret sits in the tower of her father's castle, bored with sewing, longing for adventure, and wishing not simply to find the right man but to choose him *for herself.* The man she does choose soon afterward is Tam Lin, the elfin knight thought to trap young girls. But Margaret decides to see for herself, and what she discovers is a knight living as a captive of the coldhearted Elfin Queen. When he offers her a way to help him break the enchantment, she accepts the challenge—not for the fainthearted—because she loves him.

On Midsummer's Eve, as the Elfin folk ride by, she must seize Tam Lin's fire-breathing horse by the bridle, then take his hand and hold fast to it even though the queen will change the knight's shape to frighten Margaret away. When the time comes, this means not letting go of four frightening and dangerous things: a snarling wolf, a writhing snake, a wild deer, and a burning iron bar so that Tam Lin can be reborn as the knight he was meant to be. She succeeds in bringing him to life again, as he tells her. And she does so by holding fast to what she trusts—herself and the one she loves.

Choice is the theme here; unlike the other females in her father's court, Margaret decides she has a right to choose her own prince, and she acts accordingly, just as Mairi in *The Selkie Girl* chooses to return to her life in the sea when she discovers where her husband has kept her sealskin hidden all the years of her marriage. It is not a happy choice for Mairi since it means leaving her human, landlocked children behind. But it also means that she is aware of her true nature and can be true to it. Mairi is a wild creature, so for her sense of self and personal freedom, she must choose the wild magic of the sea as her home once she finds the sealskin. One joyful result, however, is that her children can now hear her laugh for the first time.

Choice is also an important theme of Cooper's first novel after the *Dark Is Rising* sequence. *Seaward,* published eight years before *Tam Lin* and three years before *The Selkie Girl,* has for its female character a girl who is not nearly so aggressive and adventuresome as Margaret nor so independent as Mairi; yet in her own way she is learning to be less the conventional female than her world has conditioned her to be.

Seaward

Written in the early 1980s, when Cooper had just lost both parents and experienced the breakup of her marriage, *Seaward* is not the "happiest" of her books. The premise that two young adults, Cally and Westerly, can become shaman time-travelers in order to explore the individuation process, in Jungian terms, within the framework of Celtic myth and legend, produces tough going for readers. *Seaward* takes place primarily in a dream world of the psyche or the imagination or in the "otherworld" of myth; in order to create this "place" and at the same time accommodate the setting to young adult characters and the coming-of-age theme, Cooper incorporates Jungian symbols of maturation and individuation.

The book begins with Westerly, in flight from a nebulous "something" (dangerous assailants who have murdered his parents, it turns out). Standing beside a stream in an unknown land, he catches a fish with his hands, cooks it, stabs his knife into the tail bone, and says some magical words as the fish screams out; then he throws the bone into the stream before setting off once again. Soon after this, we meet Cally and her parents, who are almost immediately taken away by a tall woman with white hair and bright blue eyes. Later Cally hears her mother singing, although there is no one there. Soon the same voice turns harsh and demanding, and Cally feels "a malevolence aimed at her which somehow was retribution for everything she had failed to do"[3] (the subconscious feelings of guilt and fear that surface during the grieving process).

As she presses her hands on her mother's favorite mirror, the glass melts, transporting her into a parallel world in some ways real, in many ways very unreal. Westerly has come to the same otherworldly place but through a hidden door in the wall of the house where he lived with his mother. The enemy arrived just before this, and Westerly's mother pushed him through the wall, just before the attackers pushed into the house and shot his mother—gestapo tactics. (*Seaward* received the Janusz Korczak Award, sponsored by Jewish and Polish organizations, for a children's book exemplifying "principles of selflessness and human dignity."[4])

Both Cally and Westerly are therefore traveling to the sea on a quest to find the parents who have been taken from them. (Westerly's father, who was also taken away years earlier, is being kept on an "island," he claims.) Before they encounter one another and begin traveling together, Westerly meets a man in a golden cloak and a woman in blue who are playing chess with human figures in a flat moorland below where they stand. The board is also gold and blue (it is impossible to tell good from evil in this place; nothing is simply black and white in the game they play, the man in gold explains).

The man has tawny eyes and is likened to an owl: shades of Herne the Hunter, Arthur, and Bran. But his name is Lugan and he stands for Life, we eventually learn. (Lugh in Irish, Llew in Welsh, and Lugus in Gaulish are the names of a frequently mentioned Celtic god, according to Ellis [1994]; he was also claimed as a solar deity.) The woman in blue, Lady Taranis, who later reveals herself to be Death, is the same blue-eyed one who carried Cally's parents away. (According to McCoy, Taranis is a death goddess linked to the Otherworld.)

Readers must remain as confused and disoriented as Cally and Westerly for the duration of the journey in order to feel the displacement and disequilibrium of any traveler in a strange place. And "place" is all the more strange, since the characters are traveling inward to the psyche, filled with memories, subconscious emotions, and imaginings.

The book in some ways resembles Le Guin's *Beginning Place* (Harper 1980), another coming-of-age fantasy in which the dual protagonists, Hugh and Irena, are also fleeing something. Here it is an unhappy, impossible family life: his tormented, oppressive mother; her stepfather's sexual advances. They find a spiritual and physical happiness in a "beginning place," another otherworldly country but one unaligned with any particular culture and one perpetually in twilight. Their quest is to discover a way to bring meaning to the lives of the "ain" people, if they can only find—and slay—the dragon that threatens their existence. Less amorphous and episodic than Cooper's work, Le Guin's book contains the most distasteful image of a female—Hugh's mother and the sow-dragon that she translates into—that we are likely to encounter anywhere by a female writer. The tone and mood of Le Guin's book are so dark and oppressive that any impact the story might have is dampened considerably by the bleakness of image and character. (Coming-of-age fantasy in the early 1980s was experiencing its own growing pains.)

Cooper paints with a lighter palette, and her female oppressor, although less unconventional, is nevertheless intriguing and unpredictable. Sensing that Westerly is running from something, Lady Taranis allows him to take refuge on her chessboard. He is a pawn now, unable to see the big pattern of things that he saw before from the slope above, and he rebels against the constriction. Running away, he finds refuge with Lugan, a Merlin-Merriman figure who already knows Westerly's story (that he is searching for his father). As Westerly's "watchman" (*S*, 24), Lugan likens himself to a hawk that can intervene from the sky in perilous events. He also explains that Taranis is cruel and capricious and that this country belongs to her.

At this point Cally enters this setting to find herself among the stone "people" and a man named Stonecutter, who builds walls and, like the people, turns to stone at night, an enchantment for falling in love with a woman called Ryan, since Taranis wanted Stonecutter for herself. Taranis oppresses Stonecutter, who in turn mistreats Ryan, never praising her, never thanking her for her hard work, never smiling.

When Germanic peoples, the Teutons, began to encroach on the eastern borders of the Celts, according to Ellis (1994), the Celts referred to them as "the people." In *Seaward,* the "people" are made of stone and they build walls around others or limit their freedom just as the Germanic invaders had done to the Celts. (All time is one time, in this fantasy, or folk fantasy, where modern-day characters Cally and Westerly enter a timeless, mythic place of the past.)

Ryan lives in a stone house and appears to be obsessed with scrubbing her floor and making a checkerboard path of dock leaves on it. For as she says, "[l]ife is work" (*S,* 35). Cally will work there, too, as she discovers, when Stonecutter sends her to Ryan's house. Ryan, or "Rhiannon," as she is called by Taranis (*S,* 42), is no happy homemaker, since Taranis (Death, danger, tyranny) is constantly threatening her life. But having learned to survive in the world through subservient behavior, she teaches Cally several magical interdictions to Taranis's tyranny, one of which is the dock leaf pattern that Taranis cannot cross. (A chessboard once again appears to be a place of safety, but it merely keeps Cally in the position of the pawn, she notes from watching Ryan.)

Ryan also teaches Cally pride and independence in the face of Taranis's oppressive tactics, something very necessary for the coming-of-age theme. The separation from her parents has caused Cally's mirror reflection of herself to crack. She wonders who she is and what she is to do, and even though she tells herself she can do anything she chooses to do, she needs to know, as Ryan tells her, that she "will always have a choice" (*S,* 47). In sunlight she can leave and continue her quest; Taranis cannot hurt her then. Ryan says, "The moonlight belongs to Taranis" (*S,* 47).

The name Rhiannon is important in terms of Ryan's behavior and abilities. According to McCoy, the name translates to *divine* or *great queen* (233). Rhiannon was known in Celtic lore as a worker of magic and moon rituals. She rode a "pure white horse" (233) and appeared to Pwyll three times before he was allowed to catch her as his wife. She married him (her choice) rather than the man chosen for her, and she did so by working her magic to avoid the original match.

We find more of her story in *The Mabinogin.* There, upon the birth of a son, Rhiannon was falsely accused of killing the baby when he was stolen one night—because the ladies-in-waiting did not watch over him properly. Upon his death, they devised a ruse to rid themselves of suspicion (killing an animal and smearing blood on Rhiannon's hands). She accepted the subsequent punishment: She would carry strangers to the court on her back day after day rather than argue with the women. In

Seaward, Ryan is again given hard work to do. In both cases, Cooper's Ryan and the legendary Rhiannon, a woman is ill treated by both women and men. She has such strength of pride and courage, however, that she accepts her oppression rather than deal with female plotting or beg any man for understanding.

Ryan also gives Cally magical help in the form of the birds that will help her reach the sea if she calls upon them, just as Lugan (the hawk) will fly over the places that Westerly travels, watching over him. (According to McCoy, birds represented "transformation into the world of spirit"; they were also "co-workers in magic and ritual" [20].) Finally Ryan asks Cally, when she reaches the sea, to tell the one who will be waiting that she (Ryan) will come. The one waiting is a seal, Ryan's lover (or former husband) from her selkie world beneath the sea. As it turns out, Ryan has been tricked by Stonecutter, who wanted her for his earthly wife, and now she is simply waiting for her chance to find the sealskin and be free. When Cally asks who will be the one waiting, Ryan answers that when the time comes, Cally will know, since he will know her by her hands.

Ryan holds up her own hands at this point, and Cally sees the same growth of horn (tough, fibrous, sheathlike material) that grew on her mother's palms and grows hers, too—and on all selkie hands, she later discovers. Ryan is also called "Rhiannon of the Roane" (*S*, 42) by Taranis, the word *Roane* indicating the gray (roan) color of seals, the Gaelic name for seals, and a particular group of seal people, those of the Highlands (rather than those of Orkney and Shetland who were known as the selkies). The Roane were considered "the kindest of all fairy people" (Briggs, 136). According to McCoy, Rhiannon was also known in some stories for "singing sweetly enough to lure all those in hearing to their deaths" (234); she might therefore be related to Germanic stories of river "faeries who lured sailors to their deaths" (234). Cooper's Rhiannon is more like the traditional selkie woman who runs away from the earthly man who chooses her, in order to be with the seal husband who waits for her (the one of her own choice).

When it is almost dawn, Ryan sends Cally away from the stone house; despite Stonecutter's attempt to confine Cally in the house, as he has done with Ryan, Cally has a choice (she is still free, no human husband having tricked her to become his wife, and Taranis cannot stop her now that the moon has disappeared).

Cally and Westerly meet at the water's edge near a tower toward which they row in order to seek refuge. The place is important in two ways. Celts believed that "the river's edge, the brink of the water, was the only place where *eisce*—wisdom, knowledge and poetry—was revealed" (Ellis 1996, 24). And, in Jungian terms, the tower is "an extension of consciousness . . . a place of maturation" (Jung, 225) in which they can see what they can become or "a concretization of the individuation process . . . and a symbol of psychic wholeness" (Jung, 225).

In a cluster of tower-scenes (chapters 7 through 10), Cooper purposely uses the word *dream* five times; it is not only that Cally and Westerly are living through a waking dream such as Alice finds behind another looking glass but that, as Jung says:

> 'The dream is a little hidden door in the innermost and most secret recesses of the psyche, opening into that cosmic night which was psyche long before there was any ego-consciousness, and which will remain psyche no matter how far our ego-consciousness may extend . . . All consciousness separates; but in dreams we put on the likeness of that more universal, truer, more eternal man dwelling in the darkness of primordial night. There he is still the whole, and the whole is in him, indistinguishable from nature and bare of all egohood.' (Jung, 394)

Westerly expresses the same idea when he and Cally stand before a heavy wooden door after climbing the tower stairs: " 'Always doors. It's like one of those puzzles—a box in a box in a box' " (*S*, 56). The deeper they go into the tower compartments, the deeper they go into the puzzles of their own psyches. They find rooms with their names printed above the doors, and both rooms are the ones they had always dreamed of having. But the rooms are strikingly different.

Cally's room is airy, cheerful, and bright but barren in terms of potential for taking action in the world. It has white curtains, sunlight, a mural of sea water, gold shore, and blue sky (the chessboard colors), books, a desk, a chair, a bed, a flowered quilt, a closet filled with dresses, and a carved mirror like her mother had. Westerly's room also has books, but it is dark blue with bright stars painted overhead (Orion, the giant hunter, and the Pleiades, the seven daughters of Atlas). The room contains a model ship, glass jars, rocks, pieces of machinery, a mounted bird, a horse's skull, a "big desk set out with pads of writing-paper and a broad white sketchbook, and jars of pens and pencils and brushes" (*S*, 69), plus an artist's easel and large book written in a foreign language.

Westerly is given easel and brushes; the mural on Cally's walls is already painted. She has books to read; he has tools for writing as well.

His room is filled with avenues for self-development and exploration of the world, potential for adventures, replicas of the arts, history, language. Her room is filled with avenues for dressing up and viewing herself in the mirror. His room is outward looking; hers turns inward, a Sleeping-Beauty sanctuary: "All at once that room seemed a refuge, beckoning her with its familiar dream images" (S, 61). And whereas hers has a window, his has a door, a way to escape when Stonecutter's people come in pursuit of them to build another wall. (The male has a way out; the female is trapped within walls.)

Because this is a coming-of-age book and Cally and Westerly are dual protagonists, his room is a refuge as well. More than anything, Westerly tells Cally, he wanted to be "alone sometimes. Private . . . most of all separate" (S, 62). The rooms are dreams, he decides, since they are filled with everything they had already wanted or as Cally says, "All the things I hoped I might have one day" (S, 58). But Cally's dream-wishes are puzzling, since all that she hopes for (or can hope for) is so limited. How such a barren condition can be Cally's hope or dream is particularly puzzling, since she has nothing to do there but lie and wait or wish for something or someone to bring change into her life.

Cally calls upon the birds of Rhiannon to come and save them. When Stonecutter arrives and touches Cally, turning her to stone (a way to take another pawn in the chess game Taranis is playing with them), the birds come and restore her to life. The "rook" is no place of refuge, they see, but simply another place where they are controlled by others. Taranis, it turns out, had Stonecutter build the "tower of dreams" (S, 75) for Cally and Westerly, to keep them with her forever since, as she says, it is lonely for her in this country (the possessive parent figure). They choose otherwise.

Cally says she would rather be dead than stay where Taranis is trying to keep them. But the stone people are massed at the door, and Westerly and Cally are walled in except for a small gap (an unconventional passage) they find near the stairs. Westerly convinces Cally that there are times when you must "walk on the grass" (take the unconventional path) in order to survive, and they crawl down the passageway just in time. The sun is going down, and the stone people are bearing down on the tower, causing it to collapse on the tunnel. Resting too easy in dreams rooted in conventional thinking, like the gender-based rooms, is dangerous, Cooper appears to be saying. Your dreams can become nightmares hardened in stone: They can crumble or come tumbling down, threatening your life and even destroying you. So there is a subversive subtext undercutting the conventional role of passive, compliant female both in Ryan's story and Cally's dreams of a Sleeping-Beauty room. The conventional "wisdom" about female identity that Cally has chosen—or accepted unquestioningly—up to this point is being set up only to be demolished, just like the tower that topples behind them. (Like Taranis's chess board and Ryan's kitchen, it is not the oasis Cally and Westerly have supposed.)

Fortunately they escape into a cave, another refuge they again decide (too quickly) they will never want to leave. Here Cally meets the creature Snake, who identifies the situation in which they find themselves and the challenges life now has for them, or the purpose of their journey. At the same time, he invokes the Celtic belief in reincarnation: "Your world is all change, all journeying, and nothing that happens and no one that lives is ever lost" (*S*, 88).

Snake also awakens Cally to her selkie ancestry, " 'the folk that they call the Roane' " (*S*, 90), he says. He tells her the story of the seal who sheds her skin and then must become the wife of the man who finds it. She then sees that Ryan is Rhiannon of the Roane, a selkie. Snake teaches Cally not to succumb to the fears and guilt that pulled her through the mirror. Snake is energy, life force, confidence, and certainty, and he helps her to rejoice in life. Seducing her, he takes the pain of her grief away, and she learns in a more direct way what Ryan and Westerly have been teaching her, that there are times when one must break the rules in order to survive, attain selfhood, or personal freedom. There is, of course, a price for such freedom; in this case it is Westerly's jealousy. But Lugan appears just in time to help Westerly see the important healing quality of the sex act.

Soon they are traveling to a desert where a Charlotte-like spider called Peth helps them climb a mountain before he dies, having taught them that "each of us can do more than he knows" (*S*, 118). He also tells them that because they are young in life (able to accept, believe in, and act within the confines—or possibilities—of a magical world), they are Lugan's folk. Knowing who they are, in cultural terms, is important; soon their journey will end in a country they learn is a land of death, for it is Taranis's country, and she is Death. But Lugan, who is Life, also lives there, and Lugan and Taranis (Life and Death) are one in their resistance to one another, ruling this land of life and death together. Cally and Westerly can choose to follow their parents now to the land of Tir Na n'Og, an island where Lugan's people dwell, where people never change, and they will never grow old, Lugan tells them. But making such a choice means they will never have the chance to love one another as grown-ups, for the young there remain as they are here—*forever* young. Westerly chooses the island where his father is. Then, at the moment that Cally must choose, Ryan appears, urging her as a selkie to return to the sea. But Cally misses Westerly and this time chooses not to follow the people of Snake to their watery element. As she turns, she sees Westerly, who has changed his mind, since he too has missed her. Lugan then offers them another choice, and this one they accept: to go back to the world they left, strengthened not by the memory of this experience but by the echoes of what they gained from it. Later they will each encounter the other, and they will remember and begin their lives together then. For now, they will simply walk through the door in the rock face of the sea coast where they "could see nothing beyond it" (*S*, 167), the door signaling the Jungian "little hidden door" of the psyche, or dream state.

Thus, in this coming-of-age fantasy, we see a reflection of the Celtic belief in shamanic tradition that ordinary people as well as faerie folk could "experience a journey into nonordinary realms of existence" (Cowan, 3) or an "unseen Otherworld . . . to discover the mysteries of the divine universe" (Cowan, 7). Westerly's and Cally's choices, dreams, and reflections have made an arc of self and other that stretches from home and parents to separation from parents, to meeting of and acceptance of responsibility for one another, to separation from each other for a time.

Each young adult has also moved through three stages: impetuous behavior (Cally whistling through her teeth; Westerly turning his boat around to take her on as passenger), self-absorption (both rooms of the tower of individuation signal refuge, separation, passive or active "incubation"), and a turning outward to care about others. Each character gives up something for the other. Cally turns away from a joyous and carefree life that she would have as a seal in Snake's watery world to a life in the world from which she came and one that she will eventually share with Westerly. He relinquishes the long-awaited quest for a father in order to reenter the world and eventually resume his relationship with Cally.

There is, in other words, no refuge outside this world, no escape from it. Eventually we must face the world and whatever grief and pain come our way. Hiding, seeking refuge, running away makes us a pawn for our fears (at one point in the journey, Cally and Westerly must face—and face down—their Jungian "shadows"); the destination of our running always brings us back to ourselves. In this case, the destination of each character is the other—or the path crossing with the other.

Speaking of the young adult characters in this book, Cooper says that "they chose to go on journeying; to go back to their homeless beginnings for the sake of being able once more to meet, and to love. To connect" (*S,* 98). The "new home" they find is one another; she does not write stories that lead to home, she says: "They start there, but after that beginning part they are all journeys" (*DW,* 97), and the homecomings that follow are relationships found on the journey.

Cooper's next novel, *The Boggart,* which appeared exactly a decade after *Seaward,* shares some similarities with its predecessor. The homecoming scene of this book produces the "smashing" finale as well as most of what the book is about in terms of plot, theme, and character development. Above all, the book is about what happens when a boggart, a mysterious and clever house spirit, leaves home and makes a journey, but this journey leads back home because he finds that the new home is an impossible one. The choice he makes to go back and the courage it takes to decide to do so produces a character very different from any other Cooper character and something of a breakthrough in her writing of children's books.

The Boggart

"I wanted to write a book about an ancient creature, the trick-playing, shape-shifting boggart, who is one of the minor Old Things of Britain," Susan Cooper has said in reference to *The Boggart* (1993). "I wanted to tell the story of what might happen if a boggart were brought by chance across the Atlantic to the New World, to play his tricks there" (*DW,* 124). It was time to shift the battleground to the human world, but still Cooper did not shift her gaze from the complexities of the Old Magic to human complexities; to do so would have destroyed the hallmark of her fiction from the beginning. She simply does not separate the two planes or parallel worlds. In *The Boggart,* for the first time, she did something entirely different.

The creature, the Old Thing (the Celtic character), became one of the featured players of the story (in some ways he became the protagonist; it is certainly his fate that is at stake here) in a way that no creature of the Old Magic in her books had been before . The Greenwitch of the *Dark Is Rising* sequence is certainly an intriguing and, in some ways, a sympathetic character. But her fate is a certainty from the beginning of the book, when Jane is told about the ceremony to make a Green woman and throw her into the sea. Jane, of course, cares about the creature, and her caring spirit draws in readers to care more, too. But that concern is really, at the core, about the quest and whether it will succeed. Herne the Hunter, another Old Thing of Britain, makes a mere cameo appearance in the sequence, as does the Grey King and the afanc. But none of these creatures are, in any way, sympathetic characters, and even though Peth of *Seaward* causes us to worry about him, his fate is foreordained. He is more a Cooper invention than an "Old Thing" of folk tradition.

With the Boggart, Cooper had the perfect opportunity to create a sly, lovable, all-too-human character who elicits our amusement as well as our apprehension because we ourselves are, in so many ways, boggart-like, both as children and adults. We can see him best, in terms of Cooper's intentions and her achievement, if we remember C. S. Lewis's discussion of the animals of *Wind in the Willows:* "Are they to be adults or children?" he asks.

> You will find that they can be neither. They are like children in so far as they have no responsibilities, no struggle for existence, no domestic cares . . . In that way the life of all the characters is that of children for whom everything is provided and who take everything for granted. But in other ways it is the life of adults. They go where they like and do what they please, they arrange their own lives. To that extent the book is a specimen of the most scandalous escapism: it paints a happiness under incompatible conditions—the sort of freedom we can have only in childhood and the sort we can have only in maturity—and conceals the contradiction by the further pretence that the characters are not human beings at all . . . The happiness which it presents to us is in fact full of the simplest and most attainable things—food, sleep, exercise, friendship, the face of nature, even (in a sense) religion.[5]

It is these simple and attainable things, with the exception of, perhaps, religion, that Cooper uses to spin the web of her plot. A creature with no visible means of digesting or utilizing food loves to eat. A creature with no need of sleep or sporting events loves both. A creature with no innate desire for friendship makes one friend and then another and then two more. First, two members of his adopted Scottish family, the MacDevons, die, and he misses the humans who played with him and laughed at his mischief. Later, when he is sleeping in a rolltop desk in the Western Highlands of Scotland, and whisked off to Canada, he finds two children who warm to him and he to them.

Why do they care about him? The answer becomes the story, because here, for the first time for any of Cooper's characters, the Boggart is a developing individual, constantly surprising us—and amusing us with his startling, changeable behavior. Filled with uncommon boggart feelings, he must learn not only to recognize them but also to deal with them in the face of others' needs. He is struggling, in other words, with what defines him from deep inside and is trying to come to terms with it. He makes his own problems—and plenty for others, too (a childish thing to do), and then he does something very courageous to help solve them (a mature thing to do).

A boggart with an identity crisis? Yes, and the first of Cooper's characters to struggle with something problematic within themselves other than fear. Nearly all of her "good" characters struggle with fears of one kind or another—fear is her special subject—but these characters never abandon their essential goodness as a result of their fears, since the fears usually arise from something real—and frightening—a villain, a dangerous or puzzling event. And their response is courage in the face of danger.

"Bad" characters like Caradog Prichard, Blodwen Rowlands, Hastings, Norman Withers, the painter, or the Wiggs brothers are filled with abundant flaws (greed, overreaching ambition, self-aggrandizing urges), but they never recognize their conflicted feelings; at least we never see them doing so. They never wrestle with their defects or struggle to overcome their weaknesses to the extent that they elicit sympathy or awaken empathy. (In *Dawn of Fear,* when David Wiggs, unhappy and contrite, returns Peter's gun, Derek simply pushes him away.)

The Boggart is anything but fearful—or frightening. In fact, from the beginning, his problems arise from the opposite condition: an overabundance of recklessness and creativity, little concern for others, self-indulgence, and a general love of mischief. This is an impressive set of flaws for any character to begin struggling with if he or she is to awaken sympathy, elicit empathy, and increase narrative tension. For unlike fear, which rarely hurts or concerns anyone but the person consumed by it, recklessness can instigate dramatic conflict in the world or the death of the reckless one's spirit—if repressed.

Even better for a well-rounded children's book, the Boggart is not the only empathetic character. Cooper has created a strong cast of likable—and admirable—characters who, like the Boggart, are each struggling with some small flaw that stands to affect others if left ignored. But their struggles are as invisible as the boggart until the Boggart's conflict brings them to life.

In Scotland, Tommy Cameron's mother runs the all-purpose store across the water from Castle Keep, where the ancient MacDevon lives with a mischievous house spirit (the Boggart). Tommy is the most adult-like child in the cast—reliable, sensitive, logical. In Canada the Volnik family is composed of Robert (the father), a theater director whose outbursts of temper are so frequent no one notices them anymore; his wife, Maggie, whose negative feelings about her son's friend Barry are simmering and soon will be boiling over; their son, Jessup, whose penchant for facts outstrips his interest in feelings, as his sister, Emily, a budding environmentalist, notices. Similarly, it is her empathetic understanding that exceeds by far her understanding of technology, the very thing that will be needed to help the Boggart when he decides he must find a way to get back to Scotland. As it turns out, Barry, Jessup's friend, knows the most about technology, and he, Jessup, and eventually Tommy Cameron are the ones who save the Boggart when this irrepressible spirit places itself in life-threatening jeopardy.

For her part, Emily, when she is not busy trying to save the whales, is struggling to save herself from the self-aggrandizing tactics of a scientist who would institutionalize her in order to conduct research on an adolescent he decides is a receptor for poltergeist activity. He is unable to believe in the Old Magic and cannot therefore see that the boggart is "real." It is the scientist, who finally awakens the Boggart to the impossibility of remaining in North America, since there is no one there except the children to accept and believe in him. His tricks cannot be appreciated or even accepted as tricks if he continues to play them. And what is a boggart without tricks? Seeing his chance, he enters Jessup's computer and wills himself back home in the space game he finds there, and it is the children who trust his magic to work and who enable it to do so.

Things are easy enough for Emily, once she conquers her fears about the Boggart's safety. Next Jessup and then Tommy must give up their own desire for control. Tommy at last stops stabbing at the keyboard when the game directions announce "DANGER!" "You just have to fly,"[6] Emily has written Tommy. "Trust us," she says, and he does.

Finally, in what emerges as a master stroke for her theme, Cooper produces her grand homecoming scene for the Boggart, as Tommy lands the "plane" safely. "Giddy" and "breathless," Tommy stares at the screen, which is "quite black, save for one point of blazing blue light in the center" (*B,* 193). Intuition, magic, imagination, creativity, ingenuity, and the artistry of the Boggart are all stronger than facts, science, or technology, Cooper is intimating. It is the Boggart that is controlling the computer technology at this point, just as earlier he was able to use the "language of light" (B, 116), or the Old Magic, to advance the technology of theater lighting the day the cast of Robert Volnik's company rehearsed *Cymbeline*.

The Boggart is the strongest force in bringing about his own survival; he has made the choice, seized the moment, and placed himself into the computer after writing his message (that he wanted to go home) for them in Gaelic. He accomplished all these things despite the danger that immersing himself in the computer implied, had he been unable to escape it at the last, as he does when he finally reaches Scotland. "All at once there was a noise like a gunshot inside his computer, and it spat out the disc in an explosion of blue flame. Tommy jumped back. The disc lay on the carpet, burning and yet cold, flickering without smell or sound. Against his face he felt for an instant a cool brief touch, as if a small hand had stroked his cheek" (194).

Trust in oneself, one's intuition, and the old ways and those of the Old Things is what this book is about. Females, as Emily exemplifies, have an abundance of such intuitive trust and insight; being strong in the old ways can work for them as they do for the Boggart. It takes courage to find ways to deal with life when it becomes terribly complicated, but the Boggart shows Emily there are solutions if we trust ourselves. Then we can fly.

It also takes teamwork, friendship, and people pulling together as part of this trust. "Propped on her crutches, she [Emily] grabbed Barry's shoulder with one hand and Jessup's arm with the other" (B, 178) when the word DANGER flashed on the screen. This is not a weak female, grasping at males for support as it might seem at first glance. This is one friend supporting another, each utilizing an individual strength that the other may not have. Emily writes the long, detailed instructions to Tommy because Jessup does not like to write. Barry makes the final decision to risk the computer's crashing in order to reach the Boggart, since there is no other option. Barry is also the one who realizes that when they transfer the material to the disk to send to Tommy, there can be no backup copy. (There is no way to copy a person, he reminds them.) Since Tommy lives in the right place for the finale, his is the gravest responsibility—to play the game according to the instructions, trusting to the Boggart to know he is home and spring out of the computer at that time.

Ultimately, it takes the Boggart to trust in himself and risk dooming himself in order to do so. It is not an easy decision, as exciting as he finds the new world to be. He is enthralled with its unusual foods like pizza, its congested traffic and streetcar lines for thrilling play, the theater and backstage lighting system that he transforms into a symphony of feelings to illuminate the Shakespearean dialogue, and the wild and wonderful snowfall he discovers in Toronto. It is simply a choice that has to be made because he knows he is too different to be truly himself in the new world or feel completely at home there.

The Boggart is a metaphor for anyone who is different and misunderstood, who feels bewildered or disoriented in a new place, or who is displaced—anyone in fact like Cooper herself, a permanent alien in a foreign land. The thematic genre here is fiction of cultural displacement, fused or blended with the folk fantasy form. This in turn is merged with contemporary realism, since the Boggart, who is from another world, has entered the here and now of Emily and Jessup's world (there is no time-travel of children from one parallel world to another). Therefore, the contemporary scene is more complete and more emphasized here than in the *Dark Is Rising* sequence because the "battleground," filled as it is in this tale with complexities of magic and men in conflict, is wholly in the human world.

The Boggart is also a metaphor for the artist, the creator, the inventor, the person who stands out—and is often ostracized for seeing too much, too easily, in too many ways—or the artist giving intense pleasure to some (just as the Boggart does at the theater rehearsal), yet creating havoc for others by behaving rashly or becoming too unconventional. Thus the book is about friendship and acceptance of others *as they are*. "Whatever he had done to their lives," thinks Emily, "she loved his sense of mischief, his liveliness, his communication of delight. He was a nuisance, but he was their friend" (169).

But the book is just as much about the condition of childhood, since the Boggart is, in many ways, a child at heart; his desire to gobble up vanilla ice cream, chocolate sauce, and pizza, to play pranks, and to immerse himself in games reflects childlike behavior. *The Boggart,* in fact, shows us better what a good children's book is, filled as it is with strong, empathetic characters who struggle to believe in themselves, a tightly constructed plot, and a clever premise. It also exhibits the deftly conceived blending of genres and settings that reverberate easily against one another to produce a sharply focused theme. The book has been so well received and popular (becoming number five on the *Publisher's Weekly* Children's Bestseller List in 1996) that it is not surprising that Cooper decided to produce a companion volume.

The Boggart and the Monster

The monster of *The Boggart and the Monster* (1997) is actually a boggart. But in this case, since any boggart is also a shape changer, the monster is what became of a boggart three hundred years ago when he changed himself into a huge water-creature. He is both the legendary creature of Loch Ness (our own twentieth-century myth) as well as a cousin to the Boggart of Castle Keep, who discovers him one day when Emily and Jessup have returned to Scotland for a visit. And on a camping trip, when the Boggart has stowed away in the children's belongings and suddenly finds himself at the Loch, he remembers his lost relation and decides to make contact with him.

Deep down in the mud at the bottom of the Loch, Nessie does not respond immediately to the Boggart's greetings. When he does finally emerge from the depths, he realizes that his shape-changing abilities are horribly out of practice; he has forgotten how to be a boggart in the three centuries he has spent as a monster. Although he can shrink back to boggart size for a little while, if he forgets to concentrate or falls asleep, he finds himself expanding again to monstrous proportions, sending the scientists and tourists scurrying after the Loch Ness monster.

At this point the Boggart, filled with worry about Nessie, enters into Jessup's mind with his thoughts and memories, and Jessup learns the story of the two cousins of the Old Magic. As the pictures filter through the Boggart's mind into his own, he observes how the two of them played with the seals at the beginning, just as the Boggart does now, sometimes even taking the shape of a seal, and how the one boggart attached himself to the MacDevon family, playing his tricks for centuries. He watches as Nessie went to the Urquhart family, whose old castle is now in ruins, having burned three centuries ago (during an attack by the English, Jessup later learns). Then Jessup wakes up and informs the others that Nessie is not a plesiosaur, as their Canadian scientist friend, Harold Pindle, thinks, but merely a shape-shifting boggart. Jessup realized this in his dream when Nessie entertained the Urquhart children of old, becoming a cat, a snake, a stag, a unicorn, and finally a huge, gray monster of the Loch whenever he pleased.

What has emerged even more strongly in Jessup's dream is Nessie's loneliness, and, as Tommy, suddenly sees, the sadness the Boggart feels about Nessie's condition. Emily realizes also that the Boggart wants to do something about Nessie. Soon the Boggart is encouraging Nessie to think himself back into a boggart or to try to swim back to Castle Keep so they can live together and play with the seals. But the thought of swimming such a long distance fills Nessie with terrible fears, and he needs a great deal of urging to set off on such a quest.

The remainder of the book is taken up with how this quest is won—and how it almost is not. There is the usual conflict of believers and non-believers of the Old Magic. Here the family members of the MacDevon and Urquhart families (Jessup and Emily, plus Mary Urquhart, a spirited old lady), plus Tommy and Mr. Maconochie, the present owner of Castle Keep, are pitted against the scientists, tourists, and media people, particularly Tommy's father, a photojournalist aptly named Angus *Camer*on. And it remains for the Boggart to convince Angus that Nessie needs everyone's help to lose the shape he no longer wants and that hounding him with picture taking is only prolonging his agony.

How can Angus give up the scoop of the century? The Boggart knows, and when he and Nessie give Angus back something that he too lost in childhood—his dream of flying—Angus gives Nessie something in return, his freedom from the press. It begins with the Boggart's great idea. He and Nessie (now in boggart size) speak to Angus in Gaelic, inviting him to try flying with them. Soon Angus is running into the sky, carried by the two boggarts through the air, and realizing all the while how lucky he is to have had his lost dream of flying restored to him. Once back on the ground, he rips the film from his camera and throws it into the Loch. Now no one will know that Nessie has left Loch Ness, and Nessie can have the quiet life he wants, as a boggart with his boggart cousin.

Cooper's book this time is all about dreams, finding the truth of our dreams and bringing them to life or having the courage to do so. It is also about friendship, helping others to realize their dreams. Sometimes that means sacrificing one dream for another, as in the case of Angus, who is finally able to see the bigger picture or see beyond a selfish need in order to help someone attain freedom.

As before, the Boggart of Castle Keep is involved in a grand struggle with his own faults. For just when Nessie needs him most, the Boggart becomes distracted; then to relieve the pressure of so much responsibility in the face of his more usual condition of complete freedom, he escapes into creative trickery. He discovers Harold Pindle's underwater equipment for tracking the monster and diverts himself doing what the vehicle can never do: he imagines scenes and ideas that suddenly begin to appear as pictures on Harold's computer screen. He remembers spring; he longs for it, and suddenly flowers—a daffodil, a tulip, a white narcissus, a red anemone, and a cluster of bright blue hyacinths—appear on the screen. He wishes to be with William, the dog of Castle Keep, and suddenly William appears on the screen. Then he interprets the movement of the vehicles as a dance and creates a fancier dance for them to do.

As before, the Boggart even at his most irresponsible shows us how hopeless the computerized mind of the machine is in the face of human imagination and how magical it is to know the Boggart is out there having fun. He is the child in all of us, of whatever age, making art or living life joyously, and Cooper does not want him swept under or destroyed by technology, greed, or someone's selfish dreams. So who does she put in charge of keeping safe the Old Magic? The children, of course. Jessup, Emily, and Tommy step from the pages of the earlier book a little older this time and a little more confident and self-assured. He is *their* boggart and they understand him.

Jessup and Emily have grown a little sturdier now in their identity: they know themselves as MacDevon family members. Tommy, level-headed and logical as always and just a little jealous now of their "insider" status, nevertheless proves himself indispensable as the one who knows and can translate Gaelic, the one who is really Scottish. The young-at-heart grown-ups, particularly Mary Urquhart, are crucial to the quest, too. Mary is the Lady from the *Dark Is Rising* sequence brought to life once more but wearing blue jeans and red Wellington boots, now that Cooper has shifted the battleground to the human world. But she is equally complex and fascinating, since green eyed and mysterious, she has deep knowing of the Old Ways and the minds of the Old Ones.

Mary Urquhart still has ancestral ties to Guinevere, whose own "ancient forebears" were "green-eyed goddesses" (Goodrich, 247). Just as the color green brings to mind qualities of youth, love, and spring, Mary Urquhart runs a nursery near the Loch and sells Emily and Mr. Maconochie heather from her greenhouse. Like the Old Ones of the sequence, she knows about her visitors before they can tell her about themselves; she knew the old MacDevon and knows a great deal about boggarts, including what Nessie is feeling, because she can put her mind into his mind to help him imagine himself as small as a seal in order to swim alongside the Boggart. And she helps the others to enter more deeply into this imaging process, too. She is the Celtic shaman time-traveler, and although she herself does not become a shape changer in this story, she helps Nessie to keep his own shape as a seal more firmly in mind.

One other element is also of great help, a white fossil cockleshell that a seal throws into Emily's lap early in the story and that she keeps in her pocket as a magic talisman to help Nessie in his shape changing when unforeseen emergencies occur to take their minds off the imaging process. (At this point, Mr. Maconochie says the seal is one of the three daughters of the King of the Sea, a selkie girl; thus like to like, she was helping Emily in their quest, it is implied.)

It is Tommy who knows the seals want the fossil back; he also knows that Emily had to hold the fossil without realizing she was using it to help Nessie, an intuitive or unconscious act for which she, in particular, was needed, he decides. Again the female strength in intuition, sensitivity to others, and the ability to imagine is what is needed for a quest to succeed. The growing love and understanding that Emily and Tommy have for one another surfaces lightly throughout the book but produces the frisson at the close. Emily was needed for a different magic, Tommy tells her. (Finally Emily has her chance to save the "whales.") *We* were needed, she says in affectionate reply, bringing Tommy into the "family" of those closest to the boggart. It surely has taken a village, as Cooper has shown, to bring Nessie back, a village that is in all ways, or the best ways, a family, too. The last words, in Gaelic, are those of the two boggarts, playing this day in the shape of seals, who say in Gaelic, as Tommy translates it for her, that their hearts are with the humans.

Cooper brings her most recent book to a lyrical close, all things fitting together as closely as the five seals (the three selkie daughters and the two boggarts) that roll in and out of the waves of Port Appin. *The Boggart* and *The Boggart and the Monster* are perfect children's books for the 1990s—clever, fast paced, filled with new ideas but not overwhelmed by them or overpowering for young readers, and replete with characters we feel we know because of the way they have come to know and care about one another. They complete three decades of strong work by Cooper, and we will take a final glance at the outstanding features of her entire canon in the next chapter.

Chapter Seven
Susan Cooper as Writer

Cooper's work arises from a caldron of many influences and the confluence of several traditions; thus it results in the blending of several genres, all centered in some way around fantasy, her favorite genre. In her words, with fantasy "We aren't escaping out, we're escaping in, without any idea of what we may encounter. Fantasy is the metaphor through which we discover ourselves."[1] And for authors, she adds, "every book" becomes "a voyage of discovery" ("EIO," 16), since as fantasy writers they are "haunted by those parts of our experience which we do not understand, or even consciously remember" ("EIO," 22). As Cooper begins to write fiction, "the story [almost always] emerges as fantasy," she says. "It's as though my imagination can only find complete freedom when it's inhabiting a metaphor" ("SC" 1995, 168). But literary influence may also have something to do with it.

Literary Influences

"Certainly my unconscious rings with echoes of *Beowulf* and *The Faerie Queene, Sir Gawain and the Green Knight* and *Le Morte d'Arthur,*" says Cooper ("SC" 1996, 168). But she also remembers writing her first fantasy when she was only eight, so even earlier influences were "the fairy stories and myths and nursery rhymes" that she "absorbed" before she can remember hearing them. There were also the favorite books she read to herself. "I was a small shy spherical bookworm," she says, "and everyone gave me books as Christmas presents, though I didn't see the inside of a library until I was nine. I read myth, fairytale, legend, verse and anything else I could lay my hands on. I didn't read 20th century fantasy, except E. Nesbit, because there wasn't any."[2] Fantasy was her "country," as she says; her imagination lived there. "I'm just grateful," she adds, "that by some freak of nature I am able to write the kind of books I've always like to read" ("SC" 1995, 168).

Cooper remembers the fusion of emotion and delight, the frisson, coming from Eleanor Farjeon's *Perkin the Pedlar,* Kipling's *Jungle Books,*

Kim, and *Puck of Pook's Hill,* Elizabeth Goudge's *Henrietta's House,* Robert Louis Stevenson's *Kidnapped,* and books by John Masefield, E. Nesbit, and Arthur Ransome. Cooper reminisces, "That magical shiver of response . . . I remember feeling it certainly from the moment the children in *The Five Children and It* [by E. Nesbit] came upon the Psammead, the ancient living creature suddenly emerging from the sand after its thousand years of sleep, and certainly from the moment the young boy Kay Harker in *The Box of Delights* [1935] first meets the old man Cole Hawlings and is given that dreadful, thrilling message, 'The Wolves are running.' "[3]

Did she remember Nesbit's Psammead when she recreated her own ancient, living creature in *The Boggart* years later? Was she thinking of Kay Harker and Cole Hawlings when she invented a story about Will Stanton meeting a tramp in a lane near Dawson's farm and being told by Mr. Dawson that "the Walker is abroad . . . And this night will be bad, and tomorrow will be beyond imagining" (*DR,* 5)? Kay Harker also meets people of Old Time like Herne the Hunter, just as in another time-slip he met King Arthur and Guinevere in Masefield's earlier fantasy, *The Midnight Folk* (1927). Kay in this book also meets a lady wearing a strange ring of gold and garnets who is waiting for a message, just as Cooper will later have Will wait for a message from the Lady who wears a rose-colored ring.

Cooper's parents had a 20-volume set of Dickens, and she says it showed her "some wonderful stories, and marvelous characters . . . If I can trace any major influences on my prose style, they are Dickens, Shakespeare and the King James Bible" ("CT," 6). At age 14, Cooper encountered an anthology of verse by Walter de la Mare, *Come Hither,* that she calls "my talisman, my haunting: a distillation of the mysterious quality that sings out of all the books to which I've responded most deeply all my life—and that I dearly hope, as a writer, I might someday, somehow, be able to catch" ("NTB," 498).

The book, filled with anagrams that she has since deciphered, is about an old lady called Miss Taroone (nature or Mother Nature), living in a house in a valley in East Dene (Destiny), who reared a boy named Nahum Tarune (Human Nature). Nahum had a room at the top of an old stone tower, a room filled with shells, rocks, fossils, weapons, ship models, clocks, musical instruments, pictures the boy had painted, books, and, in particular, a book of poems with the boy's thoughts about them written in the margins.

Echoes of Miss Taroone resound in the mysterious Lady of the *Dark Is Rising* sequence (a guiding spirit, distant and aloof, telling him what he should notice and remember). Cooper might also have been thinking, consciously or unconsciously, of Nahum Tarune's room when she created Westerly's tower room in *Seaward*. And perhaps she gave the room to Westerly rather than to Cally since it had been a boy's room in *Come Hither*. However, the choice seems to be associated with aptitude or interest rather than gender: "It was the kind of marvelous room that you find described in books quite often, so often that I suspect every writer secretly hankers after it—or perhaps it's an image of the inside of any artist's mind. It was not unlike Merlin's room in *The Sword in the Stone*" ("NTB," 500).

When Cooper was at Oxford, she read *The Lord of the Rings*, and she remembers each book of Tolkien's series being eagerly awaited by the undergraduates, who were also listening to lectures by the author of these books on Anglo-Saxon literature. It was the "richly-imagined world" ("CT," 6) of these books that fascinated and may have inspired her to create a sequence of her own two decades later. Although her books are not identical in genre to Tolkien's, there is a similar emphasis on epic or high fantasy: a clash between good and evil; a quest theme and structure; integration of legendary and mythic characters; a young, innocent male blessed or burdened with an unusual fate as magical hero; and links of old and new in British past and present.

Place has its own influence in these books. Cooper walked to school past a ruin of an Iron Age fort, she says. From her home she could see Windsor Castle, built by William the Conqueror, at the same time that Bedwin brings the grail to Cornwall in *Over Sea, Under Stone*. Summer holidays in Wales meant that the part of her that was Celtic "would start singing" to her when she "heard the Welsh language" ("HWV," 27), even though, like Will in *The Grey King*, she spoke only a few words of it. "I grew up in a land of echoes," she says ("HWV," 26). The widely diverse background of Britain is reflected in the sequence when representatives of different races tell Will's brother Stephen, a sailor in the Royal Navy, when he reaches various ports around the world, that they are "ready" for the coming battle of the Dark and the Light.

British children's books, says Peter Hunt, "appeal to landscape in order to pass on national traditions and codes of conduct and to explore a national psyche."[4] Place is projected onto whatever growth patterns of character that the author is dramatizing. American fantasies, on the other hand, are more often set in secondary worlds, he adds. Living between the two cultures for the past three decades, Cooper has produced books in which there is a fusion of both, although it is probably her wide reading and creative talents that have brought about this fusion more than anything else. The secondary world becomes the real world of English place that is filled with legendary characters of Old Time. Thus she creates a genre blending of epic, time, and folk fantasy that is her own unique invention, although it is similar to the way William Mayne created the story of *Earthfasts* (1966) and Alan Garner constructed *Elidor* (1965), neither of whom she had read before creating her sequence. Thus we must cross from influence to tradition if we are to see what Cooper produces in relation to what she does with materials of the caldron once she is affected by them. How does her work resonate with that of other writers?

Literary Traditions

Several traditions flow through Cooper's fiction. Often they can all be seen at once; sometimes the stream narrows, depending on our vantage point at the particular time of reading, and we see one or two traditions in isolation. From John Masefield she draws on magic as the child's entry point into myth and legend, the magic talisman, the sense of magical delight in meeting the legendary figure (Kay and Will are both swept into Herne's world), and the child's awakening at the end of the book from a magical world. (Kay realizes it was a dream in Masefield's book; the Drew children have the magic tucked back into dreams at the end of Cooper's *Dark Is Rising* sequence.) From Nesbit she also draws on magic to set the children's adventures in motion. Cooper's children, like Nesbit's, nearly always form a society or closely knit group for "doing good deeds," as Townsend says of Nesbit (Townsend, 79).

In both the Masefield and Nesbit traditions, magic is stitched into a nearly seamless story-world, or it is so tightly integrated into the child's everyday world that the crossing from one to the other is scarcely perceptible. Kay Harker, who slips between past and present as easily as he turns the knob of the Box of Delights, is the forerunner of Will, who slips easily into the past by pressing against a handleless door. Nesbit's Psammead, who in *Five Children and It* "steals the show" (Townsend, 80), is an ancestor of Cooper's boggart, who takes center stage early in the book and never strays far from this position. In *The Boggart,* Cooper joins Nesbit's and Masefield's traditions by creating a family story with a magical creature and a magical "talisman" (the magical family adventure story). The creature, however, arises from folk legend rather than from Cooper's imagination, as Nesbit's Psammead was created, and the talisman is carved out of modern technology for a computer video game. Another tradition is one that Cooper, William Mayne, Alan Garner, Virginia Hamilton, and Nancy Bond form together, alongside Kipling and Nesbit of earlier times. These authors bring the past to life through re-created characters of history and legend with retellings and reinventions woven into the story fabric. Kipling, in *Puck of Pook's Hill*, brings literary and legendary characters from the past into the present, just as Cooper brings Merlin forward into the children's time as Merriman Lyon. Nesbit takes people from the present into the past, as Will and the Drew children often move into time-slips to meet figures of legend. The children of all these books thus function to reunite past and present time or aspects of one age or era that are missing from the other.

Such a tradition poses for readers such questions as whether the past can blend with the present. Can it continue on a steady flow into the future? (Merriman's last speech to the children hands them this legacy.) Or should the past be left behind? Does the past shape the present and future, or does the present merely absorb the past? All of the writers of the legendary time fantasy tradition touch on these questions from one perspective or another. Bond's *String in the Harp* takes up where Cooper's *Over Sea, Under Stone* leaves off, asking the question, is it right to place a priceless cultural artifact in a museum, or is it better for it to remain free in the open air or beneath the sea (nature versus culture)? So influence and tradition are united here, with Bond's protagonist, Peter, wrestling with a dilemma handed down from the Drew children's quest.

In many of these books a group of children confronts or visits the past, reflecting the notion among writers of English heritage that "British society, and the building of the Empire, required team-spirit more than individual virtue" (Townsend, 87) and among those of American heritage the premise that in union there is strength. In *Dawn of Fear*, the Wiggs family lacks this spirit. Peter and the cat that David Wiggs tortures each have an individual spirit or virtue (the cat walks alone, and Peter steps forward to stop the torturing), but neither the cat nor Peter survives and David Wiggs, the lone torturer, is at the last defeated, hated, mocked, and emotionally "leveled" by the bombing and Peter's death. In the *Dark Is Rising* sequence, it is always the group, not the individual, that is of greatest importance. The children struggle together to complete the quest; personal struggles, even characters struggling to be heroic, are de-emphasized or diminished in the face of the "bigger" picture. This is the tradition of quest adventure, high or epic fantasy, or what we might in Cooper's case call mythic fantasy.

Cooper is part of the tradition that influenced the present-day multi-volume epics for adults, as Edward Rothstein describes the narratives of "magic, prophecy and battle"[5] that evolved from J. R. R. Tolkien's *Lord of the Rings*. This group includes C. S. Lewis and his Narnia series, since in these late-twentieth-century books, we find "echoes of Christian and biblical iconography [as well as] allusions to the Arthurian legend and subtle invocations of other authors' fantasy worlds" (Rothstein, 60). Cooper's books are pre-Christian rather than "permeated with Christian imagery," Cooper says, "for the simple reason that Lewis was a devout Christian and I am not" ("HWV," 30). But there is still the strong "division between good and evil, not just as abstractions, but within the nature of man—*that* shouts out of the book" ("HWV," 30).

In the same way, although it never occurred to her to emulate ("CT," 6) Tolkien, her sequence exhibits the medieval spirit and allusions to nationality (lost kingdoms, lost powers, Dark invaders threatening the landscape, pervasive magic, wizards, and visions of a new and different age on the horizon) that infuse his work as well as that of Garner and Mayne. Will Stanton and Roland of Garner's *Elidor* are each the youngest sons, who are chosen because the older ones (adults in the world or siblings in the family) have failed to complete the required work of the quest and because they are strong, lucky, or simply destined to do the job. There are scripts, parchments, or manuscripts in each book; each is a riddle; each foretells the future. Each boy is heroic, and Will, like Tolkien's protagonists, questions his ability to be a hero. Eventually, in the case of all these children or childlike characters, however, courage, responsibility, wisdom, humility, strength, and determination work to keep the hero going and fulfill his destiny (Will's and Roland's names signal that this destiny is already in place as the book begins).

In this tradition of quest fantasy, readers encounter high purpose, eloquent language, and great status for the hero and the quest. But in Cooper's and Garner's cases, another tradition flows within or alongside this one: a parallel (rather than higher) world or dimension to which the children journey to accomplish something that will later be reflected in their own world. This brings us to the tradition of time-travel or time fantasy, in which characters of the everyday world travel back into the past or, less frequently, a figure from the past enters the character's everyday world to mingle with characters of the present.

In this tradition, there is mythic time as we see in the Narnia books (1950–56), legendary time as in William Mayne's *Earthfasts* and Nancy Bond's *String in the Harp,* historical time as in Janet Lunn's *Root Cellar* (1981) and parts of Cooper's sequence, and a blending of historical and legendary time as in Virginia Hamilton's *Magical Adventures of Pretty Pearl* (1983). Historical time divides further into near-distant time as with Philippa Pearce's *Tom's Midnight Garden* (1958) and far-distant time as with Nesbit's *Story of the Amulet* (1906). Children may also travel into the future as in Madeleine L'Engle's *Wrinkle in Time* (1962) or Virginia Hamilton's trilogy, *Justice and Her Brothers, Dustland,* and *The Gathering* (1981). They may descend into an inner psychic world of generational time, as in Hamilton's *Sweet Whispers, Brother Rush* (1982), into a dream world as in Lewis Carroll's *Alice in Wonderland* (1866) and L. Frank Baum's *Wizard of Oz* (1899), or to some combination of the two as with Jane's shaman time-traveling experience in *Greenwitch.*

Time in this tradition is an integral part of the theme. Something about time is explained or dramatized in a new way: We see life differently as a result of conceptualizing it in a particular way (the concept of time gives us new images to think with or about). Cooper's use of timeslip is more akin to that of Nesbit's in *The Story of the Amulet,* in which children simply take a magical step back in time to learn more about history, and that of C. S. Lewis, in which children take a step into a magical place outside time in order to learn more about the human joys, trials, responsibilities, and realities they will face as they grow older in actual time. Cooper's characters are, however, at the same time, filled with the fears and burdens she faced in her own childhood, growing up as she did during the Blitz of London. The children of Lewis's fantasies leave London and enter Narnia during these same war years, but they themselves are not affected by the same fears as Cooper actually experienced. Their preoccupations are focused simply on the everyday world of growing up.

In the *Dark Is Rising* sequence, time is to a great extent linked to Arthur and the idea that Arthur would, like some modern-day messiah, return when he is needed most by humans in their battles with the dark (foreign invaders). Cooper's experience in World War II and the Nazi encroachment into Europe caused her to see life in dualistic terms. Cooper explains: "[W]ar polarizes a child's view of the world. Everything becomes deceptively simple: there are the good guys, and the bad guys, Us, and Them. The good, and the evil. The enlightened, and the misguided. The Light, and the Dark" (*DW,* 145).

In many time fantasies, however, the child is working through a personal, rather than a global, problem, and entering the time warp helps to resolve difficulties. Often children like Peter in Nancy Bond's *String in the Harp* and Rose in Janet Lunn's *Root Cellar* do not feel they belong in the place where they are or do not know where they belong. (Enter the thematic genre, literature of cultural displacement.) Traveling to another time in the past helps them to accept who they are in the present. Rose says: " 'I don't want to be stuck back in time . . . I want to be myself, ordinary Rose . . . I don't belong here . . . I want to go home.' "[6] The time warp becomes a metaphor for growing. And being "stuck in time" is for Rose a way of expressing her fear of taking the next step to maturation. Once Rose realizes this, she can move on, similar to Cooper's Jane in *Silver on the Tree*.

Just as the children in *Silver on the Tree* are searching for the place where the Lady might appear with her message about the next stage of the quest, Jane balks at their moving on without knowing where they are going, until Bran speaks sharply to her about their responsibility, trying to jog her out of her disagreeable state. Soon after this, when Jane walks away from the others, she enters a time warp in which a legendary character from the past, the Lady, appears to her in a mesmerizing vision of unearthly light and color, entrusting her with the most important task of remembering the message and delivering it, despite such terrorizing interruptions as the dragon (the afanc) rising before her out of the lake. But Jane's successful delivery of the message ensures her passage through this time of adjustment. The menstrual cycle, as it is implied, is causing both her lethargy as well as her irritability; it is also signaling a change in her life pattern (her emergence from childhood).

The child who is struggling with time, identity, fitting, and growing is the one most likely to enter a time warp. For Cooper this is often the child of 12, as Jane Drew is, or near that age. Will Stanton was turning 11 when he learned he was an Old One of the Light, similar to Hamilton's character Justice in the Dustland trilogy, who learns she is a gifted seer. And both Justice and Will are members of a tradition of children coming into their extrasensory power as time-travelers of a particular culture or ethnicity, both having a shaman guide, mentor, or "old one" to help them through the magical "passage": the African-American sensitive Leona Jefferson and the Celtic, Merlin-figure, Merriman Lyon. Unlike Will, however, Justice is dealing with both a personal problem (the fear of her brother Thomas) and a world problem (the devastation of the earth from environmental abuse).

Lunn's Rose is also12. When she says she "can't ever go back" (*The Root Cellar,* 230), she means both back in time and back to childhood. Cooper's children at the end of the sequence are not allowed to go back in conscious memory to their time with the Old Ones. It must all be tucked away in the Jungian unconscious or dream time so that they can move on into adulthood, leaving magical possibilities (or "impossibilities") behind. To remember consciously would leave the child permanently displaced, unable to get back home or to find the place or time where they really belong ("stuck").

Both Cooper and Lunn know well the feelings of displacement; each has been living in an adopted country for several decades. Lunn's Rose tells a story "about a princess who could not get back to her own country" (*The Root Cellar,* 61), just as Cooper tells the story of a boggart who cannot get back to his native land. Like Dorothy in *The Wizard of Oz,* Rose and the Boggart both want to go home. There are other children's books in this tradition of characters who reinvent their ethnic and national roots on foreign shores. Frances Hodgson Burnett wrote about them; Katherine Paterson has created them. Lawrence Yep and Sook Nual Choi have done so, too. Usually the writers of this tradition are emigrants themselves or, in Cooper's case, a resident alien.

Cooper draws on more than one tradition in creating *The Boggart,* however. We have already discussed the family stories of Nesbit, the magical adventures of Masefield, and the Boggart as displaced "person." But the Boggart is above all a creature of folklore, and authors like Mollie Hunter, William Mayne, and Patricia Wrightson, before Cooper, have made a career of telling about them. Describing what Wrightson, one of her favorite novelists, does, Cooper says, "She makes her fantasies out of the relationship and conflicts between ordinary, everyday human beings and the folk-spirits of the first Australians, the Aborigines ... The real and the magical are interwoven, in the powerful landscape of that astonishing continent; these are fantasies not of good and evil but of unjudging, unjudged creatures who are, above all, *old.*"[7] If we change the words *Australian* and *Aborigine* to the word *Britons,* Cooper could be talking about her own books about the Boggart.

In these books Cooper mixes fantasy, humor, realism, and satire with folklore, magic, and information about modern technology in order to show that science is not enough; the imagination makes life more fun and also more real because it is true to the spirit. And that insight is at the heart of this particular tradition of folk fantasy, based as it is on so many genres. Genre blending is what Cooper does quite often—and does well. From her legendary-time fantasies to her folk fantasies, from her high fantasies to her coming-of-age fantasy, all of her fiction is centered in fantasy. Fantasy is how she writes, and a deeper look at her writing habits, her narrative structures, and her writing style shows us more about her creative process.

Writing Habits

Because writing has to be practiced in a "very separate private world," says Cooper, the world not of the mind but of the imagination, it is "one of the loneliest professions in the world" (*DW,* 115). Writing fantasy, she adds, is the loneliest writing of all because the writer has to go even deeper inside his or her imagination. Little daily rituals help to open the door of the consciousness. She reads chapters of what she has just written and notes made at the end of the previous day, perhaps a page of T. S. Eliot's poetry or De la Mare's notes in *Come Hither.* Or she plays with a shell, a pebble, or a ceramic artifact.

She begins her books writing in longhand; ultimately, she switches to the computer. *The Boggart,* centered on the conflict of magic versus modern technology, was written on "a lovely Macintosh," she says (*DW,* 124). She also keeps a working notebook, consisting of "detailed blueprints for books or plays" ("EIO," 19) and discussions of characters that serve to build a background for the story and a way for her to get to know her characters. She describes her notes as "cryptic and random, full of images, scattered with quotations and ideas which often seem totally irrelevant to the book at hand—though they weren't at the time" ("EIO," 19). A note might remind her that the "sword comes from the drowned land" or what she means by an image like the "opening of doors" (the "Waking of things sleeping" and the "Revealing of old things forgotten" ["EIO," 20]).

The notes are also informative for readers who may wonder what she was thinking when she created a particular setting like the Lost Land. They also show how extensive is her preparatory reading for a book. From the thirteenth-century Exter Chronica de Wallia comes her notation that the sea destroyed a kingdom of Henig, son of Glannog, called Maesmaichgen, between Cardigan and Bardssey, a stretch of land that extended up to Aberdovey. And later she tells why: "The sea level was changing in the fifth century, causing floods" ("EIO," 24).

The notations also enable us to see the truth in her statement that her books are published, not written, for children. Furthermore, like

Penelope Farmer and a number of other writers whose work is unintentionally part of the children's market (Paula Fox, Madeleine L'Engle, Rumer Godden, Joan Aiken, Scott O'Dell, E. B. White, Alan Garner, Meindert De Jong, and C. S. Lewis), she works " 'blindly and according to [her] own inclinations.' "[8] And just as she never searches deliberately for a market, she does not have her "conscious mind try to tell the subconscious what to do" ("RTB," 52). This is why to the last minute, as her notebook also reveals, "perhaps to the very last minute I shan't be sure whether he [Bran] stays [with Owen Davies] or goes [with Arthur]" ("EIO," 24).

For Cooper, getting to know her characters means opening up the doors of the unconscious to see what "image" has "snuggled down to lie in wait" there (*DW,* 124). She does not carve out her characters as a sculptor chips away at the marble, as much as she invites the characters that are already "there" to come forward, take their places onstage, and begin to play out their stories. But there are certain conscious techniques that she does appear to apply consistently in her work.

Narrative Processes, Structures, and Style

Cooper nearly always tells her story from an omniscient point of view, traveling into more than one character's mind (Barney, Simon, and Jane; Will *and* the Drew siblings; Cally and Westerly; Emily and Jessup). This is especially meaningful since it draws male and female readers equally into a book. As we saw in *Dawn of Fear,* she sometimes plays with a trio of narrative voices. Emrys Evans finds four such voices in *The Grey King.* First, there is an implied author, "propelling the narrative and addressing itself clearly and directly to the implied . . . reader."[9] Then there is the author as close observer of the Welsh scene (a more personal and intense voice) and the voices of the characters. Finally, there is what he calls a "high language, drawn from . . . what Cooper calls the High Magic, which informs the whole series" (Evans, 94). We hear this last voice in the three lords speaking to Will and Bran in Bird Rock, he notes, in the words spoken by the Grey King himself, and on certain occasions, Will uses it himself.

Although Evans focuses particularly on *The Grey King* as his example, he might as easily have chosen *Silver on the Tree,* in which variations among the voices of characters (nationality, gender, and century) swell the chorus. The function of this diversity of narrative voice is to produce reality for the mood, plot, and setting of the story and to generate a rich texture for embodiment of the theme. Evans also feels it increases the child reader's sensitivity to the way narrative works in sophisticated writing. (Cooper, he feels, can be a bridge for young readers between writers of popular culture like Enid Blyton and the narrative challenges that a writer like Alan Garner presents for child readers.)

Another narrative strategy Cooper employs is the use of myth, legend, and literary echoes for stories that characters tell to one another, of literary names for characters, and of settings that resonate with historical times and places. All of these legendary and historical allusions serve as stories within the main story, or narrative embeddings that reflect the layers of personal, social, national, and cultural identity the book is exploring. The layers of identity that time imposes on place, people, and their lives and stories often emerge as the theme of the book or at least one section of the book. Cooper's use of the name Gwion, who is the King's loyal bard Taliesin in the Lost Land as well as Will and Bran's mentor, produces a deeply layered and multidimensional identity for Gwion. He is also linked to the Dyfi salmon and is wise in the ways of Celtic magic, and all these characteristics may be what makes him one of her most appealing characters.

Her use of the mythic Green Man figure in female form in *Greenwitch* is equally intriguing; the book becomes the unfolding story of the witch, a story in the "making," since Jane, participating in the ceremony and connecting with the witch (saying "I wish you could be happy"), creates a legend of her own with herself as a character in it. But the witch is the protagonist in this story embedding. Jane knows intuitively that she herself is a creature within time, that what is important is human emotion, invested in places and artifacts, when she makes her wish for the witch to be happy. But she participates in a timeless experience, therefore escaping time. The witch changes and grows as a result of Jane's knowledge, by making her choice to give back the little case. (The witch too escapes time by participating in Jane's experience.) And the witch's mythic significance, alongside her link to a human female and her struggle with making a human choice (one that is also tied to the human quest) endows her with a many-layered identity and one that contributes to Jane's own depth of character.

Music, art, and drama all produce additional resonances in Cooper's story structures. That she has always been deeply immersed in the arts is what produces her distinctive writing style and what sets her apart from so many other writers who are publishing for children. Cooper is an imagist; she uses the language of the poetic imagination in her writing to evoke the essence of her stories. It is imagery in each of these art forms (lyric poetry, paintings in the style of Turner and Renoir, music by Mozart and Schubert, and Shakespearean drama), she explains, that brings the frisson of enchantment and evokes her best work.

Music

In *The Dark Is Rising,* music leads to the time-slip into which Will goes when he finds the wooden doors of the great hall where he meets the Old Ones of the High Magic (music begins enchantment). But it is in *The Grey King,* where the quest for the harp, as one of the Old Things of Power, takes Bran and Will on a journey to cultural knowledge. When they find the harp and bring it back, Will uses it to wake the Sleepers and then "change the world" (*GK,* 157). Later, when Caradog Prichard throws the harp into the lake as an act of vengeance on the Light, the harp at last takes on human dimensions, since, as Gwenth Evans notes, "self-sacrifice for the sake of a higher good is a repeated motif of the Dark is Rising series."[10] Yet, he adds, "there is a sense . . . that the music . . . will survive in imagination and memory" ("Harps," 208).

The scenes following the harp's "drowning" are the most musical of the book, perhaps even of the entire series. There are fluctuations in intensity, crescendo and diminuendo, in the emotional confrontation between John Rowlands and Caradog Prichard, when the "echoes of Prichard's shriek became a long howling cry through the mountains, rising, falling, rising, echoing from peak to peak, as all powers of the Dark vanished forever from Cader Idris" (*GK,* 164). There are fluctuations in time, accelerando and ritardando, in the "rustling flurrying sound that came out of the mist" (*GK,* 165) with the "great grey forms of the ghost foxes" who "came rushing headlong down the mountain" (*GK,* 165) to disappear into the dark lake, as a "cold silence" fills the valley, "save for the distant bleat" of a sheep like "the echo of a man's voice calling a girl's name far away" (*GK,* 165). The legendary aspect of the name Gwen remains unspoken but serves an important symbolic function that underscores the expressive peaks of time and intensity.

Cooper's imagination, she says, lives in the country of fantasy: "There are dragons and magicians and hobbits, a great deal of music, the paintings of [Jacques Louis] David and Claude [Lorraine] and [Marc] Chagall, and at night a starlit sky filled with comets . . . It's my refuge, this land of metaphor and enchantment" ("SC" 1988, 168). In Cooper's refuge, of which Westerly's tower room in *Seaward* is her own painted word-picture, we can imagine the paintings that both influence her artistic style or describe it best.

Art

Art historians and critics speak of the "clarity of outline," the "orderliness and elegance," and the "rich but not lavish use" of color[11] in David's work, qualities that aptly apply to Cooper's work as well. There are also references to the "lyrical quality of landscape" and the sharply focused lighting that casts "precise shadows" and "firmly realistic detail"[12] in David's paintings. In the same way, asserts Cooper, the best books for children are those in which the "story is tough, the language is precise, and the whole work is clothed—noticeably or not—in imagery" ("NTB," 506).

If Cooper "paints" her own fiction at times in the style of this artist, it may be that like David, who was "passionately engaged in the issues of his age [the French Revolution], she has been deeply engaged in the issues of her own land through time from Arthur's day, when foreign invasions were forcing a Celtic diaspora, to the era of World War II, and when Nazi aggression was producing the Holocaust. Qualities of David's art are most easily seen in *The Dark Is Rising*, especially in terms of his "sure handling of a wealth of detail [that] preserves the uncluttered speciousness of the setting" (Fleming, 440). Will's quest takes him back and forth between ornate scenes of the manor hall (culture) and the pure unadulterated worlds of winter snow and spring flooding (nature).

On the other hand, when we think of Claude and his "idyllic aspects" of landscape and his "extraordinary powers of observation" (Janson, 441), we may think of Cooper's style in *Silver on the Tree*. Here is the same "poetic essence of a countryside filled with echoes of antiquity" and the same "hazy, luminous atmosphere of early morning or later afternoon [in which] the "space expands serenely" (Janson, 441) that we see as the setting for the Drew children's quest.

Chagall's style is most easily seen in *Seaward*. His "dreamlike memories of Russian folk tales . . . and the Russian countryside" woven into a "Cubist fairy tale" (Janson, 527), as his imagination shaped and reshaped them from his childhood memories, is akin to the Jungian tale Cooper weaves from her own memories, imaginings, and reshapings of Celtic lore. But it is Chagall's uprooted, homesick, and lonely condition, living in Paris and remembering Vitebsk, that we find Cooper's strongest kinship with this artist, since in her displaced condition in America, she was writing the *Dark Is Rising* sequence and remembering winters in Buckinghamshire and summers in Wales and Cornwall. Like Chagall, whose "pictures emerged as assemblages of individual remembered moments in his life, [with] each memory [existing] in the metaphorical disguise of its own legendary overtone,"[13] Cooper also tried to preserve the nucleus of her childhood and record it, like he did, as "poetic reality, in poetic language" (Haftman, 9).

Drama

We are constantly reminded of Cooper's interest in and knowledge of Shakespeare as we read through her work, from the echoes of *Othello* and *The Tempest* in *Over Sea, Under Stone* to the tragic fury of Hawkin in *The Dark Is Rising* to the production of *Cymbeline* in *The Boggart* that forms a backdrop for the boggart's use of Wild Magic to heighten the effects of modern technology. The influence of J. B. Priestley, Cooper's friend in England, is also especially relevant to the theme of social responsibility that runs through the *Dark Is Rising* sequence, but it is especially apparent in the last book, *Silver on the Tree,* if we remember the idea of collective conscience that emerges in Priestley's play *The Inspector Calls* (1945). " 'We don't live alone,' says the Inspector. 'We are members of one body. We are responsible for each other. And I tell you that the time will come when, if men will not learn that lesson, then they will be taught it in fire and blood and anguish.' "[14]

Priestley's Eva Smith and her "hopes and fears," her "suffering and chance of happiness" all intertwined . . . with what we think and say and do" (Priestly, 56) are not so very different from what Cooper is showing in the scenes of Manny Singh, the Sikh child who is bullied by an English boy, and of the Stanton family responding to this injustice, as well as in the last speech made by Merriman, as he exits the book and his earthly existence, that it is "altogether" the children's world now, the "responsibility and the hope and the promise" is in *their* "hands" (*ST,* 272).

Cooper's experiences with drama and theater began at age three when she attended a children's pantomime and "howled and howled" ("NTB," 503) when the curtain came down. "I couldn't believe that this wonderful, magical new world, in which I had been totally absorbed, had vanished away. I wanted to bring it back again. I suppose I've been trying to bring it back again, in one way or another, ever since" ("NTB," 503). Most often she is able to bring it back through the work she does for the *Revels,* a theater company (based in Cambridge, Massachusetts, and led by John Langstaff and his daughter, Carol) that presents folk-ritual productions in prominent cities in the United States. Recruited by Langstaff, Cooper began to write plays, verse, stories, and folk-song lyrics for the Christmas Revels in the 1980s, and she has continued to do so to this day. These productions, like the books of her *Dark Is Rising* sequence, celebrate the seasons, marking "ancient landmarks in human life,"[15] she says, as well as the reawakening "echoes of winter festivals from two thousand years past: pagan and Christian, Celtic and Nordic, Anglo-Saxon and Hebrew and a dozen other cultures" ("ADR," 633). Communal in spirit, the performances involve a high degree of audience participation. "The *Revels,* like folksong and folktale," says Cooper, "is for folk" ("ADR," 637). And the nature of the material brings us to the point of *why* Cooper writes and writes so often the way she does, incorporating aspects of a "myth-haunted work" in order to fill the gap of "communal celebration" that she knows "people feel but don't quite understand" ("ADR," 637). Rituals have to be reconstructed, she might say; otherwise, they die. But this is only one of the many issues that stir her to write and to write about *why* she writes.

Authorial Vision and Thematic Issues

Cooper quotes Lucy Boston, author of the notable Green Knowe time fantasies, in explaining her own aims. Boston, whose books were often marketed for adults, spoke of never having written "down" to children; rather, she tried "to evoke that new brilliant awareness that is their world" (quoted by Cooper, *DW,* 40). Says Cooper, "The freshness of a child's vision of the world is what every artist strives to retain" (*DW,* 41). Therefore, Cooper's vision of the world is the child's vision, or at least *a* child's vision—her own.

"The child I was is the only child I really know," (*DW,* 31) Cooper wrote in 1995, quoting Ellen Raskin. "I can still feel what it was like to be that child of the 1940s from inside; I am still the same mixture of insecurity and determination, shyness and arrogance, curiosity and fear. I have the same talent she had; the same imagination. I write for her, for that child, and so it is true when I say for myself. And equally true when I say I don't write for children, not for those rows of alarming unpredictable faces. But behind the faces, there are the imaginations like mine" (*DW,* 131).

Children are "the keepers of the imagination, of the one part of us which can survive unchanged all through life" (*DW,* 131), she comments. Children will change as they travel through life but "the quality of the imagination especially in any child who grows up to be an artist [as she did] will remain a kind of talisman that links him or her to every child who will come after" (*DW,* 131). Thus the quality of Cooper's imagination is the talisman that links her to children. Writers "are all responsible for the nurturing of the imagination. Anything that lodged in our own imagination and put down roots and blossomed there . . . we can take the seed of that same image and sow it in the imagination of a child, there to blossom in the same way" (*DW,* 171).

Cooper's only agenda is to promote this imaginative link between her own experience and the child's mind. She is not trying to change children or indoctrinate them in any particular belief system; she is only sharing her experiences as they have taken root, grown, and flowered in herself. Thus the lack of any "shoulds" for females or males, old or young, beyond simply caring for one another and helping to lessen what she calls "the dreadful ubiquity of man's inhumanity to man" (*DW,* 10).

Again, the way her experience of "an incomprehensible looming menace that never went away" (*DW,* 10) informs her imagination, and it becomes the link to children. *Haunted* is the word she uses to describe the influence of the war on herself and her writing. "Whether explicitly, or through the buried metaphor of fantasy," she says in her Newbery speech, her writing "will be trying always to say to the reader: Look, this is the way things are. The conflict that's in this story is everywhere in life, even in your own nature. It's frightening, but try not to be afraid. Ever. Look, learn, remember; this is the kind of thing you'll have to deal with yourself, one day, out there" (*DW,* 10). Survival in a hard world that she herself knew well became the last spoken thought of the *Dark Is Rising* sequence, when Will tells the Drew children that they all have "a long way to go." And in her Newbery speech, she was saying that perhaps a book could help with the "long, hard matter of growing up" (*DW,* 10). How does it do so?

Cooper expanded on her notion 12 years later, saying that the writer "drops into the shadowy pool" (*DW,* 70) of children's "unconscious minds a few images" that will perhaps "echo through their lives and help them understand even improve their world, our world" (*DW,* 70). This last phrase is critical. Cooper sees the child and adult worlds as shared. Adults are not simply teaching children; children are not simply blank slates on which to be "written." Children are learning, but they are also *doing*, becoming all the time the improvers of the world they share with adults. And that is one reason why she weaves myth and legend into her stories.

America has "no one single myth" (*DW,* 70), states Cooper; it has instead many diverse, inherited "myth patterns" (*DW,* 70). Thus the need for making certain that children are aware of the archetypes that she drops into the "shadowy pool." The patterns, however, are not there to be extracted and dissected in a conscious way for child readers for an informational purpose in the classroom.

Cooper tells about a classroom in Kent, England, in which the teacher read *The Dark Is Rising* aloud to students. The school librarian wrote to Cooper that the book "became *their* book," and "their sheer enjoyment and enthusiasm spilled over into so many other things they were doing in the class, in the school and at home" ("CT," 14). They made pictures, slides, and posters, Cooper reports; they wrote poems and recorded them to music; they heard about and read the other books of the series, and they wrote letters to Cooper, telling the story of their experiences with the books. They were reading first and last for the pleasure of reading.

One of the most important issues for Cooper through the years is that children be allowed to have an aesthetic experience with literature,[16] unimpeded by adults legislating for authors how they will treat a subject. It is the writer's right, she has emphasized repeatedly, to explore the subjects of his or her particular haunting. "*{E}very child,*" she has said, "*should be encouraged to read books, words on a page, for his or her own place, in his own time, dreaming his own—and the author's—dream.*"[17]

Her thematic issues or authorial dreams have involved the quest theme, the conflict of good and evil in a perilous world, the child's struggle to overcome fear, all of which arise from what she sees as the human "longing for mythic adventure," the contemporary need for "mythic heroes" ("FRW," 310) rather than for celebrities, or the postmodernist need to ask, " 'What is a world? What kinds of worlds are there?' " and " 'What happens when different worlds are placed in confrontation or when boundaries between worlds are violated?' "[18]

Thus, her work uses what David Lodge describes as Bakhtinian "polyphony" or "dialogism" (the incorporation of many different "styles" or "voices" in a work) or, as Lodge describes, the alternation of "the narrator's voice with the voices of the characters, rendered in their own specific accents and idioms of class, region, occupation, gender."[19] Just as the postmodern novel produces a "medley of styles and voices {in which} no "ideological or moral position is immune from challenge or contradiction" (Lodge, 129), Cooper's *Dark Is Rising* sequence reveals that those of the Light, seen most clearly in the character of Merriman, are not absolved from moral and social responsibility when they become dogmatic and close minded.

There are no "black" and "white" terms where humanity is concerned, all people having the propensity for evil mixed with good. (Thus in *Seaward,* Cooper creates her chessboard colors as blue and gold.) And even though she always comes down firmly on the side of the victim, the one being bullied, oppressed, or invaded and displaced by those greedy for land or power, she also shows that there is no one way to judge the moral and social responsibility of those who are caught between the values of the Light and the Dark or the different "hues" and "intensities" of the Light. (In *The Grey King,* Gwen gives up her son, not a particularly admirable or responsible act by some standards, but she does so to gain something greater for all people of her time and place as well as for time to come.)

One of Cooper's most important thematic issues involves the relinquishing of a desired dream for a higher goal, or one affecting a greater number of people. Gwen gives up her son so that he may someday take up his father's quest for the good of mankind; Bran must accept the death of Cafall, his dog, when the needs of the quest supersede his own personal feelings; the Old Ones must see the harp go back to the waters of the Bearded Lake; the Boggart sacrifices the excitement of the New World; Tommy Cameron's father forgoes photographing the Loch Ness Monster so that Nessie can have peace of mind and freedom to play in the waters of Castle Keep; and the Drew children—on a cultural rather than a personal quest—lose all conscious memory of their adventure.

Among all these issues is the strong thematic thread of time, running through both history and myth to reveal a many-layered geographic world inside and outside time, and one that is not finished yet. Human life cannot find its fullest expression within the limits of time, Cooper's Celtic heritage reveals to her. This is an incomplete world in which dualisms cannot be resolved; we must go on learning and searching for the truth that goes on beyond this time. And the ones in Cooper's world who are doing the searching are most often children fulfilling a quest that adults cannot complete.

Unlike adults, Cooper is saying, children can believe in magic and trust their intuitive gifts. Driven by unconscious feelings and modes of conceptualizing the world, they maintain a fresh vision of things that reacquaints adults with aspects of the world that they have, in conscious memory, forgotten. Cooper's children are more open to learning and knowledge of all kinds, including intuitive knowledge; they are not weighed down by experience that closes off possibilities. In *Silver on the Tree,* when the moths fill the air around him, Will's brother Stephen forgets all that Will has told him about the conflict of Dark and Light. Having crossed the line into adulthood that precludes magical possibilities, he cannot see how any of Will's story could be true, and his disbelief, Will sees, will cause problems for the quest. So Stephen is caused or enabled to forget what he knows. (Again, what is important for the greater good supersedes individual curiosity, insight, and even learning.)

With their infinite capacity for belief, Cooper also shows, children also have an infinite variety of social actions in response to this capacity. Both Will and Jane, at different times and in different ways, fly down to the realm of Tethys; the Drew children press on in their quest despite their fears; Bran takes command when the situation demands it; Will puzzles out mysteries; Cally perseveres in her journey, keeping her promise to Ryan despite all obstacles, dangers, and nightmare visions; Cally and Westerly slip through the tower cracks to safety, just as Barney slips through a wardrobe to find a quest; Margaret trusts when few would have the courage to do so, gripping the Elfin Knight until her hands are burned. And at the end all of these children succeed, whether they are finding the Things of Power, breaking an evil enchantment, making a wise decision for the future, or flying a boggart back home.

Cooper's children are rarely angry, resentful, or even desirous of anything beyond fulfilling the quests that they discover. They are simply drawn into global conflicts that cause fear and puzzlement yet produce the children's determination to participate in an adult venture when they know they are very much needed. They grow into adulthood, immersed in conflicts that adults have caused and failed to resolve. Children are the gifted seers[20] in a universe always in danger of going wrong.

And though they live most often in fantasy settings, we know them best at times from our own mirror images. We are the children, and they are the ones we would be if we could step into the pages to share their quests. The hope Cooper gives her readers at the end of any book is that we were there and it was *well done.*

Notes and References

Chapter One

1. Susan Cooper, "Susan Cooper," *Something about the Author Autobiography Series,* vol. 6, ed. Joyce Nakamura (Detroit: Gale Research, 1988), 68; hereafter cited in text as "SC" 1988.
2. Susan Cooper, "Susan Cooper," *Children's Books and Their Creators,* ed. Anita Silvey (Boston: Houghton Mifflin, 1995), 168; hereafter cited in text as "SC" 1995.
3. Susan Cooper, "My Links with Wales," in *Loughborough '83: Proceedings of the 16th International Seminar on Children's Literature,* ed. Frank Keyse (Aberystwyth: College of Librarianship, 1983), 79; hereafter cited in text as "MLW."
4. Susan Cooper, *Dreams and Wishes: Essays on Writing for Children* (New York: Simon & Schuster, 1996), 89; hereafter cited in text as *DW*.
5. Letter from Susan Cooper, 6 January 1997 (Great Exuma, Bahamas).
6. Letter from Susan Cooper, 22 February 1997 (Los Angeles, California).

Chapter Two

1. *Over Sea, Under Stone* (London: Puffin, 1968), 74; hereafter cited in text as *OSUS*.
2. See Susan Cooper, "Preserving the Light," *Magpies* (May 1988).
3. Quoted in "Susan Cooper," *Something about the Author Autobiography Series,* vol. 6, ed. Joyce Nakamura (Detroit: Gale Research, 1988), 77; hereafter cited in text as "SC" 1988.
4. *Dawn of Fear* (New York: Harcourt Brace Jovanovich, 1970), 45; hereafter cited in text as *DF*.
5. "Muffin" in *When I Was Your Age,* ed. Amy Ehrlich (Cambridge, Mass.: Candlewick Press, 1996); hereafter cited in text as "Muffin."
6. *Silver on the Tree* (New York: Macmillan, 1977), 22; hereafter cited in text as *ST*.
7. Gillian Tindall, *New Statesman,* 2 June 1972; 760. Quoted in "Susan Cooper," *Children's Literature Review,* vol. 4, ed. Gerald Senick (Detroit: Gale Research, 1982), 44; hereafter cited in text as "SC" 1982.
8. David James, *Children's Literature in Education* (Summer 1977), 73. Quoted in "Susan Cooper," *Children's Literature Review,* vol. 4, ed. Gerald Senick (Detroit: Gale Research, 1982), 44; hereafter cited in text as "SC" 1982.

Chapter Three

1. Charlotte Spivack, *Merlin's Daughters* (Westport, Conn.: Greenwood Press, 1989), 36; hereafter cited in text.
2. *The Dark Is Rising* (New York: Macmillan, 1973), 130; hereafter cited in text as *DR*.
3. Graeme Fife, *Arthur the King* (New York: Sterling, 1991), 49; hereafter cited in text.
4. See Tom Cowan, *Fire in the Head: Shamanism and the Celtic Spirit* (New York: Harper, 1993), 111; hereafter cited in text.
5. Norma Goodrich, *Guinevere* (New York: HarperCollins, 1992), 246; hereafter cited in text.
6. Peter Ellis, *The Druids* (Grand Rapids, Mich.: Eerdmans, 1994), 111; hereafter cited in text as Ellis 1994.
7. Jacquetta Hawkes, *The Land* (New York: Random House, 1952); hereafter cited in text.
8. Peter Ellis, *Dictionary of Celtic Mythology* (Oxford, England: Oxford University Press, 1992), 222; hereafter cited in notes as Ellis 1992.
9. See Cooper's "Harvesting the Wild Values" in *Literature & Hawaii's Children,* ed. Judith Kellogg and Jesse Crisler (Honolulu: University of Hawaii and Manoa, 1992), 30; hereafter cited in text as "HWV."
10. C. C. Jung, *Memories, Dreams, Reflections,* ed. Aniela Jaffe (New York: Vintage Books, 1965), 396; hereafter cited in text.
11. Miranda Jane Green, *Celtic Myths* (London: British Museum Press, 1993), 51; hereafter cited in text.
12. Edain McCoy, *Celtic Myth and Magic* (St. Paul, Minn.: Llewellyn, 1995), 269; hereafter cited in text.
13. *Greenwitch* (New York: Macmillan, 1974), 2; hereafter cited in text as *G*.
14. Geoffrey Ashe, *The Discovery of King Arthur* (London: Guild Publishing, 1985); hereafter cited in text.
15. See William Anderson, *Green Man* (London: HarperCollins, 1990); hereafter cited in text.
16. Peter Ellis, *Celtic Women* (Grand Rapids, Mich.: Eerdmans, 1996), 221; hereafter cited in text as Ellis 1996.
17. Margaret Murry, *The God of the Witches* (New York: Oxford University Press, 1951).
18. Lloyd Alexander, "Afterword" to *Five Children and It* by E. Nesbit (1902; reprint, New York: Doubleday, 1986), 208.
19. Simon James, *The World of the Celts* (London: Thames and Hudson, 1993), 90; hereafter cited in text.

Chapter Four

1. *The Grey King* (New York: Macmillan, 1975), 7; hereafter cited in text as *GK*.

2. See *The Mabinogion,* trans. Jeffrey Gantz (New York: Penguin, 1976), 269.

Chapter Five

1. Dudley Carlson, "A Second Look: *Over Sea, Under Stone,*" *Horn Book* (19 October 1976): 522–23.
2. Keith Mano, "The Dark is Rising," *New York Times Book Review,* 22 April 1973, 8.
3. Eleanor Cameron, "Other Worlds, Other Times: *Greenwitch,*" *New York Times Book Review,* 5 May 1974, 43.
4. Jill Paton Walsh, "Evoking Dark Powers," *Times Literary Supplement,* 5 December 1975, 1457; hereafter cited in text.
5. Penelope Farmer, "Shades of Magic," *Times Literary Supplement,* 2 December 1977, 1409.
6. See Lois Kuznets, " 'High Fantasy' in America: A Study of Lloyd Alexander, Ursula LeGuin, and Susan Cooper," *Lion and the Unicorn* 9 (1985): 19–35; Susan Lehr, "Wise Women and Warriors," in *Battling Dragons,* ed. Susan Lehr (Portsmouth, N.H.: Heinemann, 1995), 194–212; and Mary Harris Veeder, "Gender and Empowerment in Susan Cooper's *The Dark Is Rising* Series," *Children's Literature Association Quarterly* 16 (Spring 1991): 11–16.
7. See Raymond Plante, "Object and Character in *The Dark Is Rising,*" *Children's Literature Association Quarterly* 11 (Spring 1986): 37–41; C. W. Sullivan, *Welsh Celtic Myth in Modern Fantasy* (Westport, Conn.: Greenwood Press, 1989); hereafter cited in text; Chris Windnagle, "The Rite of Passage in Susan Cooper's *The Dark is Rising* Sequence: The Problems of Textualized Fantasy and Fantasized Textuality," in *Literature & Hawaii's Children: Stories as Bridges to Many Realms,* ed. Judith Kellogg and Jesse Crisler (Honolulu, Hawaii: University of Hawaii at Manoa, 1992), 87–94, and Peter Goodrich, "Magical Medievalism and the Fairy Tale in Susan Cooper's *The Dark is Rising* Sequence," *Lion and the Unicorn* 12 (1988): 165–77. See also Cooper's response to these complaints ("HWV").
8. John Rowe Townsend, *Written for Children* (New York: Harper, 1992), xii; hereafter cited in text.
9. Sheila Egoff, *Thursday's Child* (Chicago: American Library Association, 1981), 307; hereafter cited in text as Egoff 1981.
10. Ann Swinfen, *In Defense of Fantasy* (London: Routledge, 1984), 229; hereafter cited in text.
11. Sheila Egoff, *Worlds Within: Children's Fantasy from the Middle Ages to Today* (Chicago: American Library Association, 1988), 20; hereafter cited in text as Egoff 1988.
12. Elizabeth Baer, "Literature for Children in a Post-Holocaust World: Evil in *The Dark Is Rising* Pentology," in *Literature & Hawaii's Children: Stories as Bridges to Many Realms,* ed. Judith Kellogg and Jesse Crisler (Honolulu: University of Hawaii, 1992), 84; hereafter cited in text.

13. Norman Holland and others, "Forum," *Publications of the Modern Language Association* III (October 1996): 1147; hereafter cited in text as "Forum."

14. Alan Cowell, "A Memorial to Gay Pain of Nazi Era Stirs Debate," *New York Times*, 29 December 1996, 11.

15. Susan Cooper, "In Defense of the Artist," in *Signposts to Criticism of Children's Literature*, ed. Robert Bator (Chicago: American Library Association, 1983), 102; hereafter cited in text.

16. Letter from Susan Cooper, 23 June 1985 (Cambridge, Mass.); hereafter cited in text as "letter 1985."

17. See J. R. R. Tolkien, *Tree and Leaf* (Boston: Houghton Mifflin, 1965), 37.

18. Letter from Susan Cooper, 23 February 1996 (Cambridge, Mass.).

19. Letter from Susan Cooper, 6 January 1997 (Great Exuma, Bahamas).

Chapter Six

1. Katherine Briggs, *Abbey, Lubbers, Banshees and Boggarts: An Illustrated Encyclopedia of Fairies* (New York: Pantheon, 1979), 142; hereafter cited in text.

2. *The Selkie Girl*, illus. Warwick Hutton (New York: Macmillan, 1986), unpaged.

3. *Seaward* (New York: Macmillan, 1983), 51; hereafter cited in text as *S*.

4. "The Hunt Breakfast," *Horn Book* (August 1984): 410.

5. C. S. Lewis, "On Stories," in *The Cool Web*, ed. M. Meek (London: The Bodley Head, 1977), 85. Originally published in *Essays Presented to Charles Williams* (Oxford: Oxford University Press, 1947).

6. *The Boggart* (New York: Macmillan, 1993, and Scholastic, 1994), 193 (Scholastic edition); hereafter cited in text as *B*.

Chapter Seven

1. "Escaping into Ourselves," *Celebrating Children's Books: Essays on Children's Literature in Honor of Zena Sutherland*, ed. Betsy Hearne and Marilyn Kaye (New York: Lothrop, 1981), 16; hereafter cited in text as "EIO."

2. "Creating the Tools," *Youth Library Review* 11 (1991): 6; hereafter cited in text as "CT."

3. "Nahum Tarune's Book," *Horn Book* (October 1980): 502; hereafter cited in text as "NTB."

4. Peter Hunt, *An Introduction to Children's Literature* (Oxford: Oxford University Press, 1994), 180; hereafter cited in text.

5. Edward Rothstein, "Flaming Swords and Wizard's Orbs," *New York Times Book Review*, 8 December 1996, 60; hereafter cited in text.

6. Janet Lunn, *The Root Cellar* (New York: Scribners, 1983), 210; hereafter cited in text.
7. "A Second Look: *The Nargun and the Stars,*" *Horn Book* (September/October 1986): 572.
8. "Address Delivered at the Children's Round Table Breakfast," *Texas Library Journal* (May 1976): 52; hereafter cited in text as "RTB."
9. Emrys Evans, "Children's Novels and Welsh Mythology: Multiple Voices in Susan Cooper and Alan Garner," *The Voice of the Narrator in Children's Literature,* ed. Charlotte Otten and Gary Schmidt (New York: Greenwood Press, 1989), 94; hereafter cited in text.
10. Gwenth Evans, "Harps and Harpers in Contemporary Fantasy," *Lion and Unicorn* 16 (1992): 207; hereafter cited in text as "Harps."
11. William Fleming, *Arts and Ideas* (New York: Holt, 1968), 438–40; hereafter cited in text.
12. H. W. Janson, *History of Art* (New York: Abrams, 1962); hereafter cited in text.
13. Werner Haftman, *Marc Chagall,* trans. Heinrich Baumann and Alexis Brown (New York: Abrams, 1984); hereafter cited in text.
14. J. B. Priestly, *The Inspector Calls* (London: Heinemann, 1992), 56; hereafter cited in text.
15. "A Dream of Revels," *Horn Book* (December 1979): 635; hereafter cited in text as "ADR."
16. See Louise Rosenblatt's *The Reader, the Text, the Poem* (Carbondale: Southern Illinois University Press, 1978).
17. "Fantasy in the Real World," *Horn Book* (May/June 1990): 310; hereafter cited as "FRW."
18. Geoff Moss, "Metafiction, Illustration, and the Poetics," *Literature for Children: Contemporary Criticism,* ed. Peter Hunt (London: Routledge, 1992), 55.
19. David Lodge, *The Art of Fiction* (New York: Penguin, 1992), 128; hereafter cited in text.
20. Virginia Hamilton, *The Gathering* (New York: Morrow, 1981), 119.

Selected Bibliography

PRIMARY WORKS

Fiction, Biography, Plays, and Essay Collections

Mandrake. London: Hodder and Stoughton, 1964.
Behind the Golden Curtain: A View of the U.S.A. London: Hodder and Stoughton, 1965; New York: Scribner, 1966.
Over Sea, Under Stone. Illus. Margery Gill. London: Jonathan Cape, 1965; New York: Harcourt Brace, 1966.
J. B. Priestley: Portrait of an Author. London: Heinemann, 1970; New York: Harper, 1971.
Dawn of Fear. Illus. Margery Gill. New York: Harcourt Brace, 1970. London: Chatto and Windus, 1972.
The Dark Is Rising. Illus. Alan Cober. London: Chatto and Windus, 1973; New York: Atheneum, 1973.
Greenwitch. London: Chatto and Windus, 1974; New York: Atheneum, 1974.
The Grey King. London: Chatto and Windus, 1975; New York: Atheneum, 1975.
Dark Encounter. Television play. 1976.
Silver on the Tree. London: Chatto and Windus, 1977; New York: Atheneum, 1977.
Jethro and the Jumbie. Illus. Ashley Bryan. New York: Atheneum, 1979; London: Chatto and Windus, 1980.
Foxfire. Play. Coauthored with Hume Cronyn. First produced at Stratford, Ontario, 1980. New York and London: Samuel French, 1983.
Seaward. New York: Atheneum, 1983; London: Bodley Head, 1983.
The Silver Cow. Illus. Warwick Hutton. New York: Atheneum, 1983; London: Chatto and Windus, 1983.
The Dollmaker. Teleplay. Coauthored with Hume Cronyn. Produced by American Broadcasting Companies, Inc., 13 May 1984.
The Selkie Girl. Illus. Warwick Hutton. New York: Macmillan, 1986.
Foxfire. Teleplay. Produced by Columbia Broadcasting System, 13 December 1987.
Matthew's Dragon. Illus. Joseph A. Smith. New York: Macmillan, 1991.
Tam Lin. Illus. Warwick Hutton. New York: Macmillan, 1991.
The Boggart. New York: Macmillan, 1993; London: The Bodley Head, 1993.
Danny and the Kings. Illus. Joseph A. Smith. New York: Macmillan, 1993.

Dreams and Wishes: Essays on Writing for Children. New York: Simon & Schuster, 1996.
"Muffin," in *When I Was Your Age: Original Stories about Growing Up,* ed. Amy Ehrlich. Cambridge, Mass.: Candlewick Press, 1996.
The Boggart and the Monster. New York: Simon & Schuster, 1997.

Essays, Articles, Speeches, and Edited Collections

Essays of Five Decades, by J. B. Priestley, ed. Susan Cooper. Boston: Little, Brown, 1968; London: Heinemann, 1969.
"A Love Letter to the *Horn Book.*" *Horn Book* (October 1974): 182–83.
"Address Delivered at the Children's Round Table Breakfast," *Texas Library Journal* (May 1976): 52–54.
"Newbery Award Acceptance." *Horn Book* (August 1976): 361–66.
"Susan Cooper." *Fourth Book of Junior Authors and Illustrators,* ed. Doris de Montreville and Elizabeth Crawford. New York: H. W. Wilson Company, 1978, 98–99.
"A Dream of Revels." *Horn Book* (December 1979): 633–40.
"Nahum Tarune's Book." *Horn Book* (October 1980): 497–507.
"Escaping into Ourselves," in *Celebrating Children's Books: Essays on Children's Literature in Honor of Zena Sutherland,* ed. Betsy Hearne and Marilyn Kaye. New York: Lothrop, 1981, 14–23.
"In Defense of the Artist." In *Signposts to Criticism of Children's Literature,* ed. Robert Bator. Chicago: American Library Association, 1983, 98–108.
"My Links With Wales." *Loughborough '83: Proceedings of the 16th International Seminar on Children's Literature,* ed. Frank Keyse. Aberystwyth, Wales: Welsh National Centre for Children's Literature, 1984, 79–81.
"Introduction." *The Christmas Revels Songbook: In Celebration of the Winter Solstice,* ed. John and Nancy Langstaff. New York: David R. Godine, 1985.
"A Second Look: *The Nargun and the Stars.*" *Horn Book* (September–October 1986): 572–74.
"Susan Cooper." *Something about the Author Autobiography Series,* vol. 6, ed. Anne Commire, 67–85. Detroit, Mich.: Gale Research, 1988.
"Preserving the Light." *Magpies* 2 (May 1988): 5–9.
"Fantasy in the Real World." *Horn Book* (May–June 1990): 304–15.
"Susan Cooper." *Something about the Author Autobiography Series,* vol. 64, ed. Anne Commire, 75–85. Detroit, Mich.: Gale Research, 1991.
"Creating the Tools." *Youth Library Review* 11 (1991): 6–8, 10–14.
"Harvesting the Wild Values." *Literature and Hawaii's Children: Stories as Bridges to Magic Realms,* ed. Judith Kellogg and Jesse Crisler. Honolulu: University of Hawaii, 1992, 22–33.
"Susan Cooper." *Children's Books and Their Creators,* ed. Anita Silvey, Boston: Houghton Mifflin, 1995, 168.

SECONDARY WORKS
Books

Egoff, Sheila. *Thursday's Child: Trends and Patterns in Contemporary Children's Literature.* Chicago: American Library Association, 1981. Discusses Cooper as an important fantasist in children's literature who places her protagonists on the "edge" between real and fantasy worlds, Darkness and Light, dream and memory, known and unknown, order and chaos (a precarious situation).

―――. *Worlds Within: Children's Fantasy from the Middle Ages to Today.* Chicago: American Library Association, 1988. Discusses Cooper as epic fantasist who places child protagonists in universal rather than personal struggles for identity.

Spivack, Charlotte. *Merlin's Daughters: Contemporary Women Writers of Fantasy.* New York: Greenwood Press, 1987. Discusses Cooper alongside nine other female fantasists; cites Cooper for her superb stylistics, complex narrative structures, vision of time, and use of Celtic myth.

Sullivan, C. W. *Welsh Celtic Myth in Modern Fantasy: Contributions to the Study of Science Fiction and Fantasy.* New York: Greenwood Press, 1989. Studies the influence of Celtic materials on six authors of High Fantasy; asserts that Cooper uses Celtic sources to intensify the affective power of her stories.

Swinfen, Ann. *In Defense of Fantasy: A Study of the Genre in English and American Literature since 1945.* London: Routledge and Kegan Paul, 1984. Studies Cooper alongside other fantasists such as Tolkien, Lewis, Alexander, Le Guin, and Farmer, who evaluate the real world through the construction of fantasy and bring new insight to the notion of myth.

Townsend, John Rowe. *Written for Children.* New York: Harper Trophy, 1992. Discusses Cooper in terms of imagined worlds; sees *The Dark Is Rising* as the best book of the five.

Articles and Parts of Books

Baer, Elizabeth. "Literature for Children in a Post-Holocaust World: Evil in *The Dark is Rising* Pentology." In *Literature & Hawaii's Children: Stories as Bridges to Many Realms,* ed. Judith Kellogg and Jesse Crisler. Honolulu: University of Hawaii at Manoa, 1992, 77–86. Asserts that adults have a stronger concept of evil after the Holocaust and that children's literature and Cooper's books are needed to warn readers about this situation.

Corbett, Linda. " 'Not Wise the Thought—A Grave for Arthur.' " *The ALAN Review* (Fall 1993): 45–48. Sees the *Dark Is Rising* series as an important springboard for students conducting research on the Arthurian legends.

Deifendeifer, Anne. "Susan Cooper." In *Children's Books and Their Creators*, ed. Anita Silvey, 169. Boston: Houghton Mifflin, 1995. Brief overview of Cooper's life and work.

Evans, Emrys. "Children's Novels and Welsh Mythology: Multiple Voices in Susan Cooper and Alan Garner." In *The Voice of the Narrator in Children's Literature: Insights from Writers and Critics*, ed. Charlotte Otten and Gary Schmidt. New York: Greenwood Press, 1989, 92–100. Sees *The Grey King* as the most accomplished of the five books and discusses four narrative voices that emerge in it.

Evans, Gwenth. "Harps and Harpers in Contemporary Fantasy." *Lion and the Unicorn* 16 (1992): 199–209. Discusses harps used by many children's writers drawing upon Celtic legend to reveal national character or show growth of personal character.

———. "Three Modern Views of Merlin." *Mythlore* 62 (Summer 1990): 17–22. Examines use of Merlin in Tennyson, Powys, and Cooper, in whose work Merriman (Merlin) has ties to Tolkien's Gandalf.

Goodrich, Peter. "Magical Medievalism and the Fairy Tale in Susan Cooper's *The Dark Is Rising* Sequence." *Lion and the Unicorn* 12 (December 1988): 165–77. On the function of medieval settings, characters, and subjects in Cooper's *Dark Is Rising* sequence; asserts that the values central to Cooper's books, medieval romance, and modern fantasy are strength (of body and will), courage, loyalty, freedom from oppressors, and wisdom.

Greenlaw, Jean. "Books in the Classroom." *Horn Book* (November–December 1988): 820–33. Relates how in a three-month study of fantasy, she used Lloyd Alexander's and Cooper's books.

Hunt, Peter. "Landscapes and Journeys, Metaphors and Maps: The Distinctive Feature of English Fantasy." *Children's Literature Association Quarterly* 12 (Spring 1987): 11–14. On the journey motif as organizing factor for children's fantasy, with layers of history in the landscape deepening the texture and the literary image of England, if the writer is faithful to the "map" of a particular English place.

Kuznets, Lois. " 'High Fantasy' in America: A Study of Lloyd Alexander, Ursula LeGuin, and Susan Cooper." *Lion and the Unicorn* 9 (1985): 19–35. Examines high fantasy series of Alexander, Le Guin, and Cooper in terms of the Arthurian theme of male development.

———. "Susan Cooper, a Reply." *Signposts to Criticism of Children's Literature*, ed. Robert Bator. Chicago: American Library Association, 1983, 109–13. Response to a talk Cooper gave at the 1977 Children's Literature Association Conference, in which Cooper attacked Freudian critics and those who take an "issues" approach to the evaluation of children's books. Asserts that the reader has a right to ask questions about how and why authors are revealing the world.

McElderry, Margaret. "Susan Cooper." *Horn Book* (August 1976): 367–372. Discusses how Cooper's gifts of writing came to be; her influences include music, legend, poetry, theater, imagination, intellect, and a strong sense of time, people, and place.

Plante, Raymond. "Object and Character in *The Dark Is Rising.*" *Children's Literature Association Quarterly* 11 (Spring 1986): 37–41. Asserts that fate controls the events in the *Dark Is Rising* sequence, and this lessens the impact of theme and diminishes the importance of individual choices that characters make.

Roose-Evans, James. "Susan Cooper." *Twentieth-Century Children's Writers,* ed. D. L. Kirkpatrick. New York: St. Martin's Press, 1978, 305–6. Appraises the books of the *Dark Is Rising* series, finding *The Grey King* the best.

Rosenfeld, Judith. "Books in the Classroom: Tales of King Arthur." *Horn Book* (July–August 1992): 501–6. Describes classroom experience of children reading stories about King Arthur, including Cooper's *The Grey King,* to uncover why the stories are still popular today.

Stephens, John, and Susan Taylor. " 'No Innocent Texts': The Representation of Marriage in Two Picture-Book Versions of the Seal Wife Legend." *Young Readers, New Readings,* ed. Emrys Evans. Hull, England: Hull University Press, 1992, 99–122. Report of a study in which Australian students responded in terms of social values embodied in Cooper's *The Selkie Girl;* says the loss of the mother at the end became the element of crisis for readers.

Veeder, Mary Harris. "Gender and Empowerment in Susan Cooper's *The Dark Is Rising* Series." *Children's Literature Association Quarterly* 16 (Spring 1991): 11–15. Asserts that Cooper's fiction is limited by marginalized females and the patriarchal mode; Jane is a conventional and powerless female. Employs Freudian criticism to uncover phallic symbols in Miss Greythorne, the afanc, the manuscript case, and the horns of Herne.

Windnagle, Chris. "The Rite of Passage in Susan Cooper's *The Dark Is Rising* Sequence: The Problem of Textualized Fantasy and Fantasized Textuality." *Literature & Hawaii's Children: Stories as Bridges to Many Realms,* ed. Judith Kellogg and Jesse Crisler. Honolulu: University of Hawaii at Manoa, 1992, 87–94. Theorizes that since the Arthurian, Celtic past cannot be found (it is lost in an ancient oral tradition), it must be reinvented by fantasists like Cooper.

Index

Alexander, Lloyd, 48
Arthur the King: in historical accounts, 4, 40, 79, 133; in medieval romance, 63–64; as Pendragon, 8–9, 72. *See also* Cooper, Susan: Celtic lore in works; works, *Dark Is Rising* sequence

Baer, Elizabeth, 84–85
Bawden, Nina, 15, 89
Bond, Nancy, 124, 126–27
Boston, Lucy, 89, 135

Campbell, Joseph, 34
Caws, Mary Ann, 90
Chagall, Marc, 132–34
children's literature, 38; compared to adult literature, 25; compared to literature of child culture, 15–16, 21–23; identifying qualities of, 51, 89, 115
Children's Literature Association, 95
Cooper, Ethel Field (mother), 1
Cooper, John Richard (father), 1
Cooper, Rod (brother), 5
Cooper, Susan: awards for writing, 49, 76, 102; brother, 5–6; censorship of work, 85; childhood, 1–3, 16, 122; childhood experiences with theater, 134; childhood reading, 120–21; children, 5–6, 48; college, 3–4, 122–23; cross-cultural heritage, 5–6, 128; development as writer, 2–3, 6, 76, 119; divorce, 5, 101; grandparents, 1; literary influences, 120–23; marriage and family life, 4–5, 16; parents, 1–2; point of view in writing, 16, 21; reader reactions (adults), 22, 77–85, 96–98; reader reactions (children), 86–89; remarriage, 5; Shakespeare, minithesis at Oxford, 3; vision of world, 2–3, 23, 40, 77–79, 93, 137–38; Wales, as important influence in writing, 1–3, 49, 129

ARTISTIC TALENT
depth of character, 93, 115
emotional resonance, 93–95
empathetic characters, 88–95, 112
evocation of scene, 89, 91–93, 96
experiments with language, 59, 91–92
originality of ideas, 26, 41, 59, 118–19
storytelling power, 11, 26, 46, 58, 113–14

CELTIC LORE IN WORKS
beliefs about: birds, 32–33, 105; glass, 66, 69, 81; habitat of gods, 35; horse's skull, 67; salmon, 65; transmigration of souls, 24, 69, 108–9; trees, 41, 67; water, 29, 35, 65, 106
Druids, 8, 28, 42, 73
festivals, 41, 52
folk creatures: boggart, 110–19; jumbie, 99; selkie, 100, 105, 108
legendary figures: Arthur, 7, 58, 64, 69; Blodeuwedd, 71; Guinevere, 27, 57, 63, 81–82, 118; Merlin, 8–9, 122; Rhiannon, 104; Taliesin, 69
legends: Grail Knight, 48; Grey King, 52; Guanhumara, 27, 81; Gwenhuyfar, 81–82; *Mari Llwyd,* 67–68; Phantom ship, 46; Wild Hunt, 36–37
mythic figures: Bran, son of Lir, 51; Elffin, 69; Danu, 81; Grail King (Fisher King), 48, 64; Grail Knight, 48; Green Man, 42; Gwenhywyvar, 27; Gwyddno, 69; Herne the Hunter as death deity, 37; Janus, 27; Juno, 63, 82; Lugh (Llew, Lugus), 102); Mother Goddess, 27, 63, 81; shaman shape-changers, 29, 34, 39, 43–44, 101, 119, 126; Taranis, 103
omens, 29
rituals, 81

CELTIC LORE IN WORKS (*continued*)
symbols: Guinevere as Mother goddess, 27, 82; mandala of immortality, 25, 34–35; mistletoe of fertility, 73; Mother Goddess of Knowledge, 27; oaken doors as entry to spirit world, 26; salmon of wisdom, 65; sea as supreme female, 81
verse-chant prophecies, 33, 48, 53
women in Celtic society, 81–82

GENRES IN WRITING
child culture, literature of, 15–16, 21
cultural displacement, literature of, 115, 127
dual audience, literature of, 38
fantasy, 6, 120, 129; coming of age, 101–3, 107, 109; epic, 79; folk, 99, 104, 115; High, 6, 125; legendary time, 25; mythic, 38, 70, 125; science fantasy, 7; time-travel, 78, 125
fictional autobiography, 16
genre-blendings, 16, 38, 128

IMAGES AND SYMBOLS IN WORKS
chessboard/chess game as quest pattern, 31, 65–66, 102–4, 107
child as quest figure, 138–39
colors: blue, 46, 53, 55–56, 58, 69, 102–3; blue and gold, 64, 102, 106, 138; tawny (eyes of birds), 37, 50, 71, 102
doors, 26, 106, 109; music as door to spirit world, 60, 62, 92
grail, 9–10, 14, 25
leaping salmon, 65–66, 69
magical birds, 59, 105
mandala, 25, 30, 35, 61
mirror, 66–67, 102
mistletoe, 73–74
Things of Power, 37, 51, 68

LITERARY CRITICISM OF WORKS
cultural studies: feminist readings, 14, 46–48, 76, 80, 100–101, 107; cultural history, 81–85; issues approaches, 85

gendered readings, 94
genre theories, 79–80
Jungian theories: anima, 82; dreams, 128; individuation, 68, 101–2; unconscious, 75, 83–84
liberal humanist tradition, 49, 77–79
myth-in-literature, 80
personal criticism, 90–98; personal vs. traditional, 90
reader response studies, 86–89, 91

NARRATIVE PROCESSES USED IN WORKS
dreams and intuitions, 75
intersecting narrative voices, 20–21
legendary names, 57, 69, 71–72, 125, 131–32
literary "echoes," 131; Arthurian lore (*see* Arthur the King); *Beowulf,* 11–12; *Burnt Norton,* 11; *Come Hither,* 121–22; *Cymbeline,* 114–15; *Five Children and It,* 7, 48; *Just So Stories,* 17; *Le Morte d'Arthur,* 57, 81–82, 132; *Mabinogian,* 27, 54, 71, 104; *Othello,* 14; *Peter Rabbit,* 17, 19–20; *Sword in the Stone,* 8; *Tempest,* 11, 54
metaphorical embeddings, 91–92
musical language, 92
mythical blendings: Gwen/Guinevere, 63; Gwion/Taliesin, 69, 131; Gwyddno/Grail (Fisher) King, 64; Jane/Juno, 63
mythical inventions: Bran, son of Arthur and Gwen/Guinevere, 57; Greenwitch, 41; Lady, 81–82; Lugan, 102; Taranis, 102–3
story embeddings, 69, 91–93, 131
time-slip devices, 124, 126; *Dark Is Rising,* 25–26, 132; *Greenwitch,* 46, 126; *Grey King,* 54, 57–58; pictorial time-slip, 91; *Silver on the Tree,* 59, 61–62, 64, 67, 70, 72, 74

THEMES AND SUBJECTS OF WORKS
bully who must be stopped, 18–19, 134
child's initiation to evil, 20
choices influenced by social responsibility, 37, 109–10, 114–15, 131

INDEX

conflict of good and evil (Light and Dark) in perilous world, 26, 57, 72, 80, 84, 87, 126
cultural quest: for good of world, 36, 40, 49, 134; for grail, 13–14; for harp 51; for self knowledge, 64–65; for Signs, 26, 31, 34
dreams: brought to fruition, 117; sacrificed for higher good, 132
fear, 112; courage in face of danger, 94, 82, 109, 112, 139; as legacy of war 17; of sheltered female, 82; struggle to overcome, 137; of unknown, 62, 66–67, 126
female with freedom to make choices, 101, 104–5, 109
fierce caring producing loving bonds, 36, 93, 95, 97
friendship: as acceptance of others, 115; as helping others to realize dream, 117
imaginative spirit stronger than technology, 113–14, 117
irrationality of evil, 19
loving bonds as strongest force on earth, 74, 93
need for fierce caring in world, 36
personal quest: to find parents, 102; to go home, 110, 117
time: all time as one, 71, 104; linked to Arthurian period, 126; as travel into history or to magical place, 126–27; as unfinished history and myth, 131, 138
war affecting child's world, 20

WORKS, DARK IS RISING SEQUENCE
Arthur as character, 9, 13, 15, 45, 61, 73–74
Arthurian legend, use of, 126
celebration of seasons, 135
compared to *The Boggart,* 115
evocation of scene as major strength, 90
group struggle, theme of, 124
history of creation, 15, 24–25
literary strengths of individual books, 77–79

reader reception, 76, 86–89
social responsibility, theme of, 134, 138

WORKS, NONFICTION
Behind the Golden Curtain, 4
Dreams and Wishes: Essays on Writing for Children, 3
Essays of Five Decades, 5
"In Defense of the Artist," 95
J. B. Priestley: Portrait of an Artist, 5
"Newbery Medal Acceptance" (1976), 136

WORKS, NOVELS
Boggart, The, 5, 6, 110–16, 119, 121, 123, 128–29
Boggart and the Monster, The, 6, 116–19
Dark Is Rising, The, 24–39, 76, 80, 81–82, 86, 89, 118, 123, 132–33, 137
Dawn of Fear, 5–7, 110–16, 119, 121, 123, 128–29
Greenwitch, 25, 39–48, 76, 78, 80, 81, 86, 93–98, 126, 131
Grey King, The, 25, 49–59, 76–79, 81, 100, 122, 130, 132, 138
Mandrake, 4, 7
Over Sea, Under Stone, 7–15, 18, 24–25, 76, 78, 86, 94, 122, 124
Seaward, 101–11, 122, 132–33, 138
Silver on the Tree, 24, 59–76, 78, 80, 82–84, 91, 93, 95, 127, 130, 133–34, 139

WORKS, PLAYS AND TELEPLAYS
Dollmaker, The, 5
Foxfire, 5

WORKS, SHORTER FICTION
Danny and the Kings, 100
Jethro and the Jumbie, 99
Matthew's Dragon, 100
Selkie Girl, The, 100, 101
Silver Cow, The, 100
Tam Lin, 100–101

WRITING
childhood and adolescent, 3–4
early adulthood, 4–5, 7
feelings about child audience, 16, 136–39
habits, 129–30
influence of art and drama in, 131–35
literary traditions in: folk fantasy, 128; legendary and historical fantasy writing, 124–26; literature of cultural displacement, 127; magical family adventures, 123; multivolume epics, 125; quest adventure, 124–25; time travel, 125–27
plays and teleplays, writing style, 131

Cronyn, Hume, 5, 89

David, Jacques Louis, 132–33
De La Mare, Walter, 121, 129
de Troyes, Crétien, 63
Dickens, Charles, 121

Egoff, Sheila, 77
Eliot, T. S., 11, 129
Evans, Emrys, 130

Farmer, Penelope, 99
Field, Frederick Benjamin (maternal grandfather), 1
Field, Mary Ellen Davies (maternal grandmother), 1
Flores, Richard, 91

Garner, Alan, 123–25, 130–31
Geoffrey of Monmouth, 40
Grant, Jonathan Roderick (son), xiii, 5, 6
Grant, Katherine Mary (daughter), xiii, 5, 6, 48
Grant, Nicholas, (first husband), xiii, 4
Guinevere, Arthur's Queen: as cross-cultural heroine, 73; in medieval romance, 57, 63, 81–82. *See also* Cooper, Susan, Celtic lore in works

Hamilton, Virginia, 124, 126–27
Hawkes, Jacquetta, 5, 32, 44
Holland, Norman, 90
Hunt, Peter, 122
Hutton, Warwick, 100

Jung, Carl, 68, 75, 106; anima theory, 82, 109; individuation theory, 83, 101–2, 106, 128

Kipling, Rudyard, 17, 120, 124
Kroeber, Karl, 90

Langstaff, John, 135
Le Guin, Ursula, 103
Lewis, C. S., 3, 9, 111, 125–26, 130
Lively, Penelope, 15, 89
Lodge, David, 127
Lorraine, Claude, 132–33
Lunn, Janet, 126–28

Malory, Thomas, 63
Masefield, John, 120–23
Mayne, William, 123–26
McElderry, Margaret, 21–22
Modern Language Association, 90

Nesbit, Edith, 7–9, 12, 48, 121, 123–24, 126

Pearce, Philippa, 89–126
Priestley, J. B., 5, 32, 134; *The Inspector Calls* (play), 134

Raskin, Ellen, 135
Revels (theater company), 135

Sanderson, Derek, 86–89, 94–96
Shakespeare, William, 3, 11, 14, 54, 114–15, 134
Smith, John Wayland, 37
Smith, Lillian, 77
Spivack, Charlotte, 79–80
Stairway to Heaven (motion picture), 1
Sullivan, Charles W., 79
Swinfen, Ann, 77

Tandy, Jessica, 5, 89
Tolkien, J. R. R., 3, 95–96, 122, 125
Townsend, John Rowe, 77–78, 123

White, T. H., 8
Wrightson, Patricia, 89, 126

The Author

Nina Mikkelsen received her Ph.D. in English from Florida State University and has completed postdoctoral work in children's literature at Ohio State University and the Columbia University School of Library Science. She has taught at universities in Florida, North Carolina, and Pennsylvania. Her research interests are in children's and young adult's responses to literature, cross-cultural literature, American and African-American folk literature, ethnic fiction, narrative processes and traditions, and time fantasy for children and young adults. Her essays have appeared in *Canadian Children's Literature, Children's Literature Association Quarterly, English Journal, Journal of Youth Services in Libraries, Language Arts, New Advocate,* Scribner's *Writers for Young Adults,* and *Touchstones* (vol. 2). She is the author of *Virginia Hamilton* (Twayne, 1994).

The Editor

Ruth K. MacDonald is college dean for the I Have a Dream Foundation in Hartford, Connecticut. She received her B.A. and M.A. in English from the University of Connecticut, her Ph.D. in English from Rutgers University, and her M.B.A. from the University of Texas at El Paso. She is the author of the volumes on Louisa May Alcott, Beatrix Potter, and Dr. Seuss in Twayne's United States Authors and English Authors series and of the books *Literature for Children in England and America, 1646–1774* (1982) and *Christian's Children: The Influence of John Bunyan's "Pilgrim's Progress" on American Children's Literature* (1989).